AF443169

ACES OF THE EIGHTH

FIGHTER PILOTS, PLANES & OUTFITS OF THE VIII AIR FORCE

by:
GENE B. STAFFORD
WILLIAM N. HESS

squadron/signal publications

If you have photographs of the aircraft, armor, soldiers or ships of any nation, particularly wartime snapshots, why not share them with us and help make Squadron/Signal's books all the more interesting and complete in the future. Any photograph sent to us will be copied and the original returned. The donor will be fully credited for any photos used. Please send them to: Squadron/Signal Publications Inc., 1115 Crowley Dr., Carrollton, TX 75006.

COLOR KEY

Olive Drab	Gray	Natural Metal	White
Red	Yellow	Green	Antiglare Green
Blue	Dark Blue		

PHOTO CREDIT:

This book would have been impossible without the cooperation and help of a number of people. The organizations deserving thanks are the Air Force Museum, the Air Force Archives, the National Data Records Center and the Magazine and Book Branch at the Department of Defense. We would also like to thank the following individuals: Robert Ammon, Clarence Anderson, Donald Baccus, Ernest Bankey, Walter Beckham, Wayne Blickenstaff, Robert Booth, Donald Bryan, Leonard Carson, William Clark, Merle Coons, Mrs. Claude Crenshaw, George Cueleers, George Doersch, Urban Drew, Glenn Duncan, Ralph Englehart, Royal Frey, Gary Fry, Francis Gabreski, Francis Gerard, David Glover, Art Hieden, Wallace Hopkins, Art Jeffrey, Ralph Johnson, Robert Johnson, John Landers, William Lewis, Charles London, Walker Mahurin, Danny Morris, James Morris, Merle Olmstead, Peter Pompetti, Dave Robinson, Ken Rust, Wilber Scheible, William Smelzer, Everett Stewart, Donald Strait, William Tanner, David Thwaites, Jerre Vleit, David Weatherill, William Whisner, Sidney Woods, and Hubert Zemke.

Ferocious Frankie
GUN CAMERA

ACES OF THE EIGHTH

In March 1943 the skies over occupied Europe were dominated by an experienced and confident Luftwaffe. Many of the German pilots were veterans of more than three years of aerial warfare against first rate opposition, and even the inability of the Germans to bring the Royal Air Force to its knees in the Battle of Britain had not dampened the morale of the men. There had been some drain on the air power on the Western Front to meet the needs of other fronts, but this drain had been almost insignificant in terms of total strength. The Germans were much more concerned with the nocturnal bombing raids of the RAF than the feeble attempts of the Americans to mount a daylight bomber offensive.

Both of the great air powers in Europe had tried daylight bombing and had found that it led to excessive losses for the attacking force. It was only natural to believe that the American philosophy of precision daylight bombing would run on to the same hard rocks of reality that had forced the Germans and the British to seek the relative safety of darkness for bombing missions. The major problem was the inability to protect the bombers from concerted attacks by fighters.

Across the narrow stretch of water from Occupied Europe, three fledgling American fighter groups, the nucleus of **VIII Fighter Command,** were about to be commited to combat. Of these, only the **4TH** had combat experience. This unit had been formed the previous fall from the Americans flying with the RAF in the three **"Eagle"** squadrons.

All three outfits were equipped with a first line fighter in the P-47 but, unfortunately, the plane was still not available in the needed quantities. The Thunderbolt suffered the same malady that plagued RAF and Luftwaffe fighters — insufficient range to protect the bombers all the way to the target and then back home. What the young American pilots lacked in experience, equipment and tactics, they made up for in enthusiasm, a desire to learn, and a strong conviction that they were just as good as the enemy pilots. Unfortunately, desire could not bring down an enemy plane nor enthusiasm protect a bomber formation. As a result, the first few months of fighter operations by the **Eighth Air Force** proved more than a little frustrating. The three units took a good bit more punishment than they gave during this period.

As time passed the Eighth Air Force evolved and grew and eventually became the largest single air organization the world had ever seen. The hard learned lessons of the spring and early summer of 1943 provided the much needed experience and tactics for survival. New men, machines and units flowed into the battle. By the end of 1944 the number of fighter groups in VIII Fighter Command had risen to fifteen and each of these was almost double the size of the original three. Deficiencies in equipment were overcome as improved versions of the Thunderbolt arrived on the scene along with P-38 Lightnings and P-51 Mustangs.

The growth in the number of operational fighters in the Eighth Air Force is shown in Figure 1. The P-47 and P-38 made up the bulk of the strength for the first year of action but both were eventually supplanted by the P-51. In 1945 only one group, the 56TH, was equipped with anything but the North American product. The

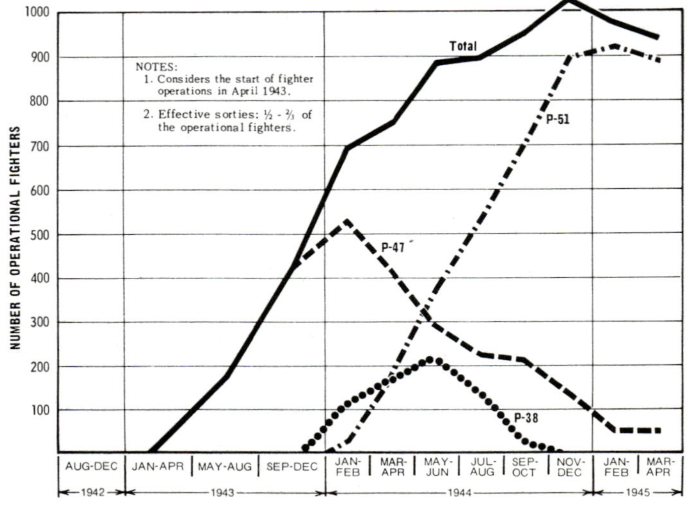

FIGURE 1 — EIGHTH AIR FORCE FIGHTER STRENGTH

actual numbers of fighters put up at any one time usually ran one-half to two-thirds of the operational number. The remainder of the aircraft were not required, held in reserve, or experienced some mechanical difficulties.

The range of the Mustang and the Lightning was good, but even so there was a desire to extend it. With the Thunderbolt, the range was perhaps the biggest drawback to the fighter. The bombers had to penetrate to Berlin and beyond to hit targets and the fighters had to provide escort if the losses were to remain within acceptable limits. The answer to the range problem came with the use of drop tanks for the fighters. As the size of these tanks grew during the war, so did the range of the aircraft. Figure 2 shows the escort range for all three fighter types at various stages in the war. If the fighters operated independently of the bombers, the range was even further increased since the planes didn't have to use gas by weaving back and forth over the heavies. In this type of operation the Thunderbolt could operate well beyond Berlin in the later stages of the war.

flying skill and background. Desire, ability, leadership and even a certain amount of luck entered the equation but whatever the qualities, the men in this book had them. Perhaps, after all, that is really all that needs to be said.

Both air and ground victories were credited by the Eighth Air Force but for this book only those gained in the air have been considered. This is not meant to demean the achievements of those pilots that scored against ground targets since these victories were often more hazardous than the ones in the air. The major reason for the decision is to allow the scores to be compared with pilots of other air forces that didn't include ground scores. The exception to this rule is found in the section on the **339TH Fighter Group.** In order to include the normal complement of photos, it was necessary to include men who scored ground victories.

Though the Eighth Air Force and its component elements have been the subject of more books and magazine articles than any other American air organization, coverage has often been limited to the better known aces and

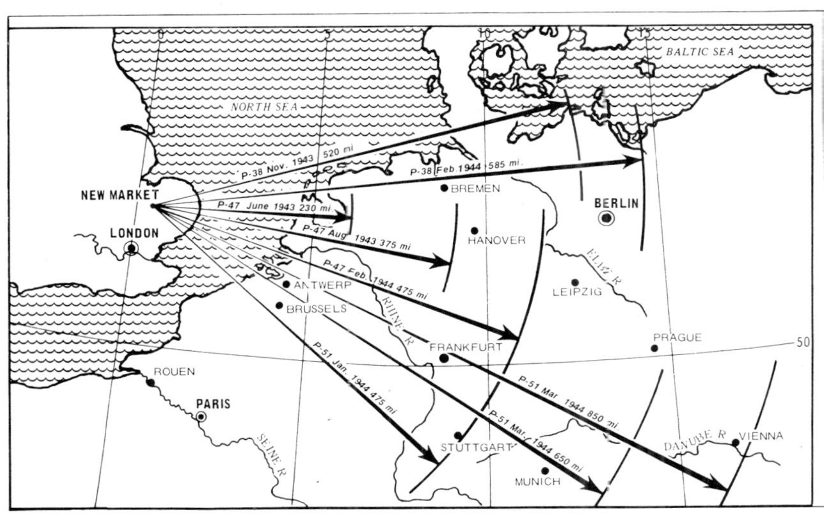

FIGURE 2 — EIGHTH AIR FORCE FIGHTER ESCORT RANGE

Machines and organizations are important ingredients in the recipe for aerial victory but in the final analysis it is the man in the cockpit that ultimately decides victory or defeat. Upwards of 5,000 fighter pilots served with the Eighth Air Force during its more than two years of fighter operations. Of these, however, only a relatively small number succeeded in downing five or more enemy planes in combat and earned the title: **"ace".** This book is dedicated to this small, elite circle of men and to the units in which they served.

No attempt has been made to analyze the many factors that go into the making of an ace. This has been the subject of much scholarly debate and, in fact, is still a subject of vital interest to the Air Force some half century after Alan Wilkensen became the first American ace back in the First World War. The aces of the Eighth Air Force were of every size, temperament,

outfits. As a result, such men as Gabreski, Bob Johnson, Preddy, Meyer, Gentile, Carson and their planes are rather well known to most people with an interest in World War II aviation. The same cannot be said for the great majority of the aces of the Eighth. The top aces of the lesser known outfits and even some of the high scorers with the better known groups are not widely known.

When the research for this book was started the goal was to include photographs and text on the top several aces from each of the fifteen fighter groups in the Eighth Air Force. Though this goal has been approached, it has not been reached. With the passage of time the remaining gaps will be filled and the coverage expanded so that all of the aces and their aircraft can be portrayed. This will have to wait for sequels to this volume.

GENE B. STAFFORD
WILLIAM N. HESS

4th Fighter Group

The **4TH Fighter Group** was the only American unit activated in an active combat theater. This took place on 12 September 1942 when the three Eagle Squadrons of the RAF (71, 121 and 133) were officially transferred to the USAAF. Thus the Group had the distinction of being the oldest Group in the Eighth Air Force. The outfit operated from Debden throughout its entire combat career with the Eighth. The first combat mission flown in American colors was on 2 October 1942. The Group entered combat flying the Spitfire but in March 1943 converted to the P-47. The outfit switched mounts again, this time to Mustangs, in February 1944 and continued to fly the P-51 throughout the rest of the war. The 4TH was the first Eighth Air Force fighter group to penetrate German air space (28 July 1943) and the combined total of ground and air victories led all other units in that category. It received the Distinguished Unit Citation for its actions during the period of 5 March to 24 April 1944. In this less than two month period the Group destroyed 189 German planes in the air and 134 on the ground. By the time the 4TH Fighter Group had flown its last mission on 25 April 1945, some 583½ enemy planes had fallen before its guns in the air and 469 more had been destroyed on the ground. The Group lost 241 aircraft during its 2½ years of service.

Squadron Codes ● 334th - **QP**, 335th - **WD**, 336th - **VF**

(Above & opposite page top left) DON S. GENTILE (21.84) - Gentile's hometown was Piqua, Ohio. He joined the RAF prior to America's entry into World War II and was assigned to 133 "Eagle" Squadron. Two of his victories were scored before the outfit was transferred to the USAAF. On 8 March 1944, he was credited with the destruction of 4¼ German aircraft and on 29 March he scored a triple. Gentile scored doubles on five other occasions. An earlier aircraft was named "Donnie Boy" and was coded VF☆P (Credit: USAF, G. Fry).

DUANE W. BEESON (19.3) - Beeson called Boise, Idaho home and he was also a former member of the RAF (71 "Eagle" Squadron). He was downed by flak on 5 April 1944 and spent the rest of the war as a POW. His P-51B, shown here, was coded QP☆M and bore the serial number 43-6819. An earlier P-47 carried the QP☆B code and was named "Boise Bee" (42-7890) (Credit: W. Hess).

JAMES A. GOODSON (15.) - A native of Toronto, Canada, he was a veteran of service with the RAF. Goodson scored two of his victories while on detached service with the 15TH Air Force. His 15 ground victories put him near the top of the strafers. Goodson went down on a strafing mission and was captured on 20 June 1944. The codes on his aircraft were VF☆B (Credit: USAF Museum).

RALPH K. HOFER (16.5) - Salem, Missouri was Hofer's hometown. He came to the 4TH by way of the RCAF and on his first mission with the 4TH scored a victory. He was killed in action on 2 July 1944 while on a shuttle mission. "Salem Representative" was coded CP☆L (42-106924). A P-47 of Hofer's also was coded QP☆L but the name of the plane was "The Missouri Kid" and "Show-Me" (Credit: G. Fry).

JOHN T. GODFREY (16.3) - Though born in Canada, Godfrey was raised in Rhode Island. As with many 4TH pilots, he served with the RAF before joining the Group. Among his victories was a triple scored on 22 April 1944. Godfrey was shot down and taken prisoner but after two unsuccessful attempts, he finally escaped from POW camp. The aircraft shown here was coded VF☆P (43-6765). As can be seen, this ship was not named "Reggie's Reply" as has been reported (Credit: Godfrey).

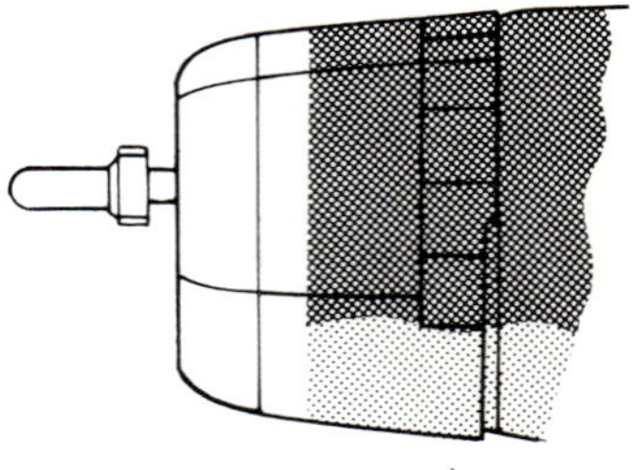

24 inch white band for all aircraft

DONALD J.M. BLAKESLEE (15.5) - Another veteran of the RAF, Blakeslee hailed from Fairport Harbor, Ohio. He served as the commander of the 4TH from January to November 1944. Three of his victories were scored with the RAF and another while Blakeslee was flying with the 357TH. His aircraft were coded WD☆C but they carried no personal markings (Credit: W. Smelzer).

FRED W. GLOVER (10.34) - Glover left his hometown of Asheville, North Carolina to fly with the RCAF after he was turned down for service in the USAAC. He finally joined the 4TH and rose to command the 336TH Squadron. Among his victories was one over an Me-163 on 2 November 1944 and a triple on 21 November 1944 (Credit: W. Smelzer).

PIERCE W. MCKENNON (12.) - **While strafing an airfield, McKennon was forced to bail out. George Green landed in the same field and after both pilots disposed of their chutes, Green sat on McKennon's lap and flew the pair home. The man in the shot was a professional golfer on a visit to the Group. McKennon's plane carried the codes WD ☆ A (44-14221) (Credit: E. Stewart).**

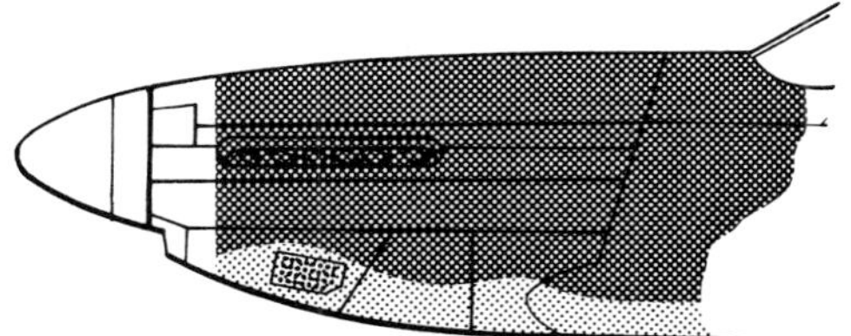

White spinner & 12 inch white band used until late March 44.

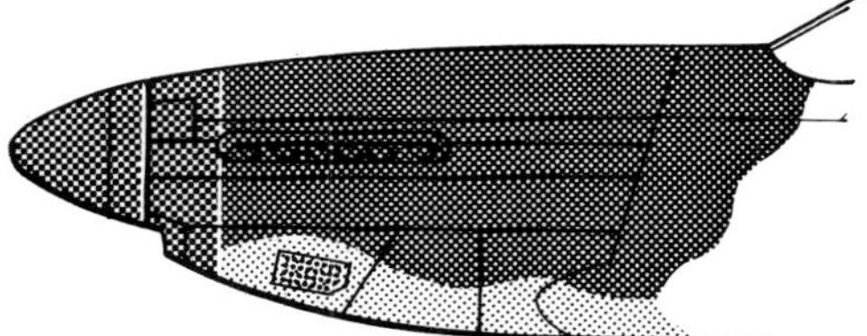

Red spinner & 12 inch red band from late March 1944.

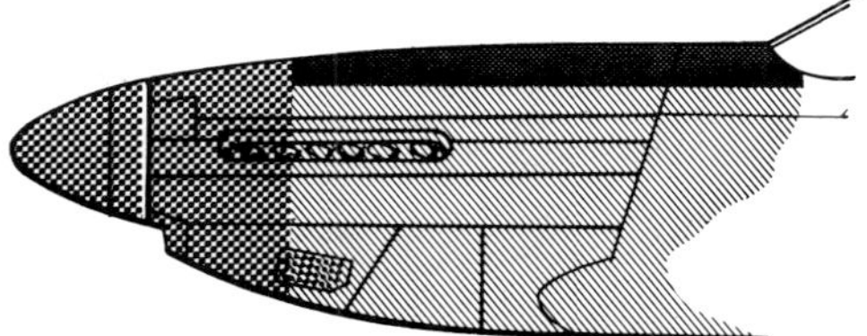

Red band extended to 24 inches from December 1944.

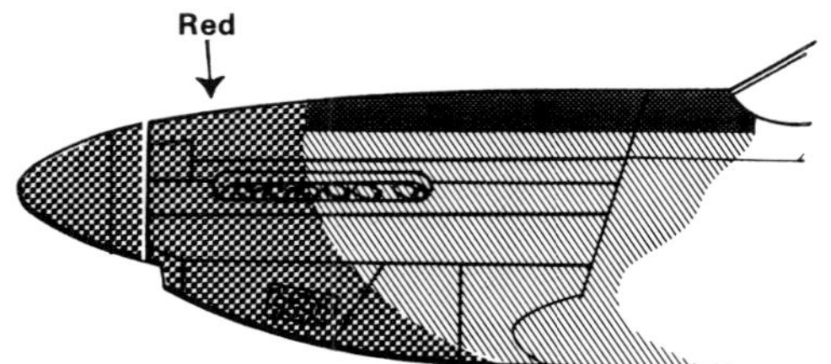

Red band swept back and down from January 1945.

ACES

NAME	SCORE	OTHER GROUPS
Don S. Gentile	21.84	RAF
Duane W. Beeson	19.3	
Ralph K. Hofer	16.5	
John T. Godfrey	16.3	
Donald J.M. Blakeslee	15.5	RAF
James A. Goodson	15.	15th AF
George Carpenter	13.3	
Willard W. Millikan	13.	
Howard D. Hively	12.	
Pierce W. McKennon	12.	
Nicholas Megura	11.84	
James A. Clark, Jr.	11.5	
Louis H. Norley	11.3	
Charles F. Anderson	10.5	
Frederick W. Glover	10.3	
Ted E. Lines	10.	
Sidney S. Woods	10.	49/479
Bernard L. McGrattan	8.5	
Albert L. Schlegel	8.5	
Claiborne H. Kinnard	8.	355
Joseph L. Lang	7.84	
Everett W. Stewart	7.83	18/352, 355
Vermont Garrison	7.3	
Spiros Pissanos	7.	
Joseph H. Bennett	6.5	56
Paul S. Riley	6.5	
Raymond C. Care	6.	
Kendall E. Carlson	6.	
Roy W. Evans	6.	359
David W. Howe	6.	
Henry L. Mills	6.	
William E. Whalen	6.	
Oscar H. Coen	5.5	
Michael G.H. McPharlin	5.5	RAF/339
Hipolitus T. Biel	5.5	
Richard Becker	5.	
Van E. Chandler	5.	
Frank C. Jones	5.	
Jack G. Oberhansly	5.	78
Carroll W. McColpin *	11.	RAF/9th AF
William J. Daley *	8.	RAF/9th AF
Gregory A. Daymond *	7.	RAF
Chesley G. Peterson *	7.	RAF
Gerald C. Brown *	5.	55
Selden R. Edner *	5.	RAF

* All victories with other units

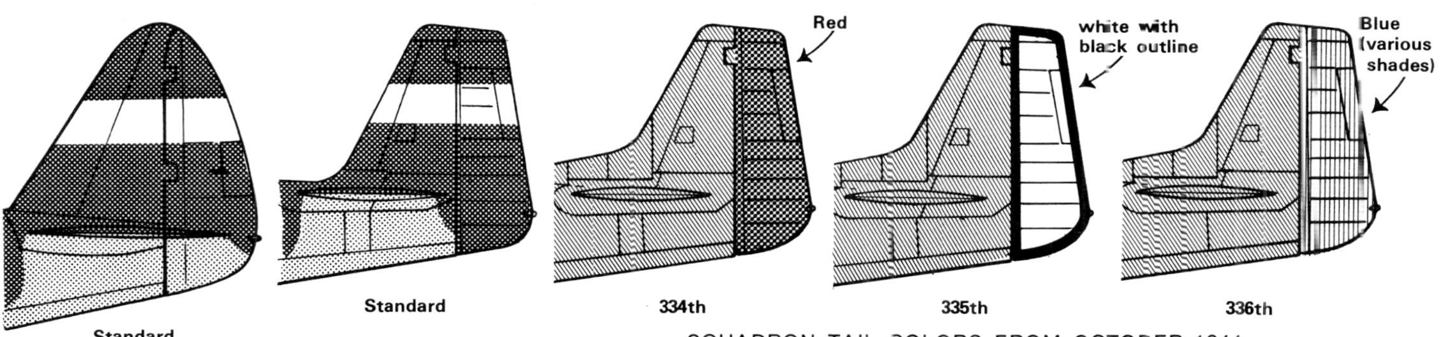

SQUADRON TAIL COLORS FROM OCTOBER 1944

20th Fighter Group

The **20TH Fighter Group** was the oldest fighter group assigned to the Eighth Air Force on a long term basis. Though the roots of the Squadrons went back to World War I, the Group was activated on 15 November 1930. When war was declared in 1941, it served as a training ground for the new groups forming rapidly. It also served as part of the air defense structure on the West Coast before shipping out for England. On 25 August 1943, the 20TH arrived at Kingscliffe Air Base, the home of the outfit for the entire war. The first Group combat mission was flown some four months later on 28 December. The individual Squadrons had flown as a fourth Squadron to the 55TH Fighter Group on separate occasions prior to this however. Although assigned to bomber escort duties, the 20TH also took on the fighter-bomber role beginning in March 1944. After this time activities were almost evenly divided between the two types of missions. The many successful attacks on rail transportation by the Group gave rise to its nick-name: "The Loco Busters". The original mount for the 20TH was the P-38 and it continued to fly the Lightning (H and J models) until July 1944 when new P-51Cs began to arrive. As the war progressed, the Group converted to D-model Mustangs and ended the war flying the P-51K. In the course of some 312 combat missions, the 20TH Fighter Group destroyed 212 German planes in the air and an additional 237 on the ground. The Group lost 132 planes to enemy action.

Squadron Codes ● 55th - **KI**, 77th - **LC**, 79th - **MC**

(Above and right) JACK E.M. ILFREY (8.) - Ilfrey's hometown was Houston, Texas. Before joining the 20TH, he had served with the 1ST Fighter Group and five of his victories were scored with the North Africa based outfit. One of his victories with the 20TH was rather unusual. On 24 May 1944, he had just shot down one Me-109 and was beginning a turn when another of the German fighters bore in from straight ahead. The two planes collided and Ilfrey's wingtip was shredded. Ilfrey was able to nurse his crippled P-38 home but the German was not so lucky. His P-38, "Happy Jack's Go Buggy" was coded MC ☆O (4338431). His later P-51 may have also been coded MC ☆O (Credit: USAF).

ERNEST C. FIEBELKORN (9.5) - Fiebelkorn, a native of Lake Orion, Michigan, was one of the largest fighter pilots to see action in the ETO. At 6-4 and 225 pounds, it was quite a struggle to wedge himself into the cockpit of his P-51. Though his combat tour started at a slow pace, he ended the war as the top gun in the 20TH Fighter Group. He scored a triple on 2 November 1944 and shared in the destruction of an Me-262 on 8 November of the same year. The victory was scored while he was flying LC☆N (44-11161). This plane may have been "June Nite". Another of his planes was LC☆F and it is this ship that is shown on the color plate (Credit: W. Smelzer, W. Hess).

JAMES M. MORRIS (7.3) - Jim Morris called Detroit, Michigan home. All of his victories were scored in the P-38 and he was one of the top scorers in the ETO in this type. His biggest day came on 8 February 1944 when he downed two FW-190s and two Me-109s. On 7 July 1944 Morris was in the process of downing an Me-410 when the German plane shot him down. He parachuted from his stricken craft and spent the rest of the war as a POW. Contrary to popular opinion, he never flew "Black Barney". This was Col. Barton Russell's plane. His four victory day came while he was flying LC☆G (42-67871) but the plane he called his own was "My Dad". This ship was coded LC☆E (42-67717) ("Til we meet again" appeared on the starboard side of the nose) (Credit: J. Morris).

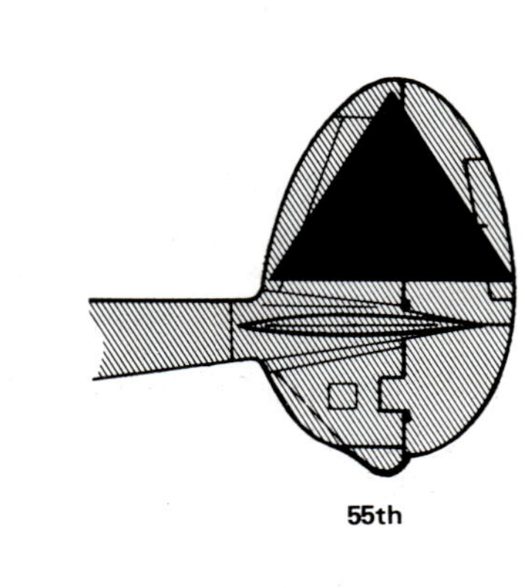

55th

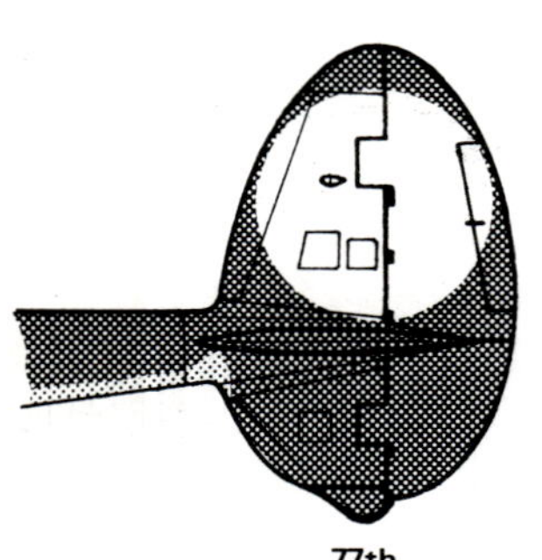

77th

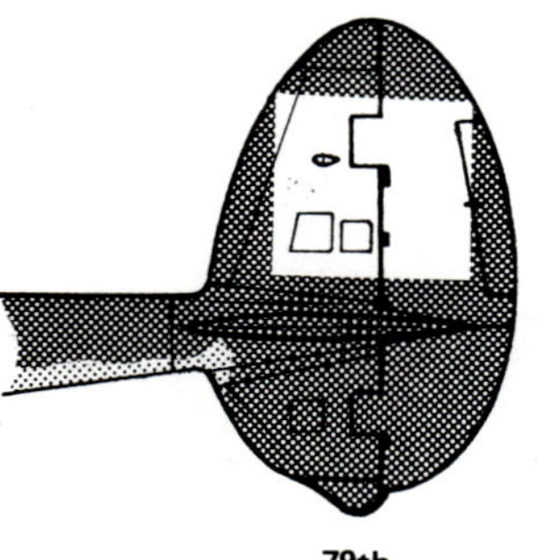

79th

HARLEY L. BROWN (6.) - Brown, a native of Wichita, Kansas, joined the 20TH in August 1944 and completed his tour in March 1945. His biggest day came on 2 November 1944 when he downed two FW-190s and an Me-109. He flew P-51s coded KI☆N (44-13779) and KI☆A (44-11250).

LINDOL F. GRAHAM (5.5) - Graham was the second man to make ace in the 20TH Fighter Group. His biggest day came on 18 March 1944 when he scored a triple. He scored his last victory on the day he was killed. Graham had followed an Me-110 down to the deck and just after the German plane bellied in, Graham made one last pass but as he pulled up he went into a roll, nosed down and went straight into the ground. His P-38, "Susie" was coded MC☆L (42-67926) (Credit: R. Englehart).

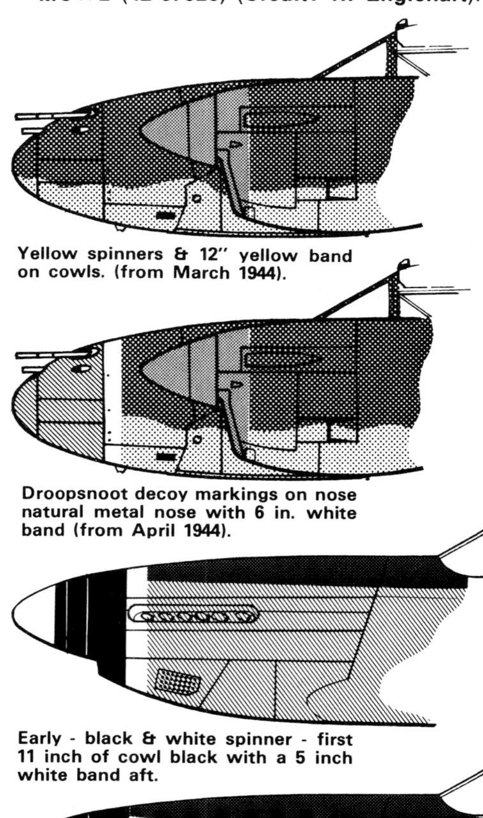

Yellow spinners & 12" yellow band on cowls. (from March 1944).

Droopsnoot decoy markings on nose natural metal nose with 6 in. white band (from April 1944).

Early - black & white spinner - first 11 inch of cowl black with a 5 inch white band aft.

Late - black & white as shown. White area sometimes left in natural metal.

ACES

NAME	SCORE	OTHER GROUPS
Ernest C. Fiebelkorn	9.5	
James M. Morris	7.3	
Harley L. Brown	6.	
Lindol F. Graham	5.5	
Jack E.M. Ilfrey *	8.	1
Joseph T. McKeon *	6.	475
Jack C. Price *	5.	78

* Victories primarily with other units.

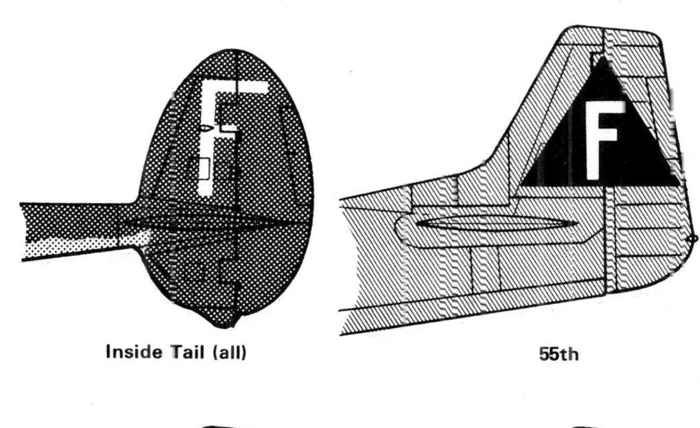

Inside Tail (all)   55th

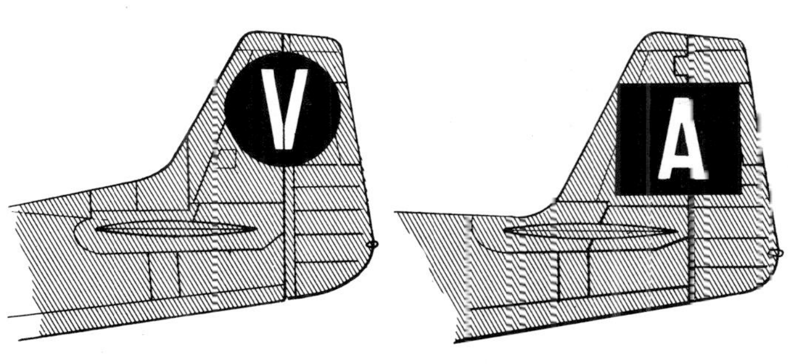

77th   79th

55th Fighter Group

The **55TH Fighter Group** was activated at Hamilton Field, California on 15 January 1941. In several moves on the West Coast during the training period, the Group lost two of its original squadrons but by the time the unit headed for Europe in September these had been replaced. The 55TH settled into its home, Nuthampstead, on 16 September 1943. The unit used this base until 16 April 1944 when it moved to Wormingford. The unit remained there throughout its remaining tenure in England. The 55TH was the first P-38 outfit in the Eighth Air Force and flew this type of aircraft until 19 July 1944 when it began operations with the Mustang. The honor of flying the first Eighth Air Force plane over Berlin fell to the 55TH. The Group received a Distinguished Unit Citation for eight missions during the period 3-13 September when it destroyed a large number of enemy planes in the air and on the ground. A second DUC was awarded for operations on 19 February 1945 when the unit flew a sweep over Germany to hit transportation targets. The first Group mission was flown on 15 October 1943 and some year and a half later when the unit flew its last mission the scoreboard read 316½ aerial and 268½ ground victories. The 55TH lost 181 planes during this period.

Squadron Codes ● 38th - **CG**, 338th - **CL**, 343rd - **CY**

ROBERT E. WELCH (6.) - **Welch, a native of Brown City, Michigan, got most of his victories during the Fall of 1944. Among his victories was one on Christmas Eve 1944. This particular German didn't even wait to be shot; he went over the side as soon as Welch got on his tail. His last victory came on 17 April 1945. (Credit: W. Smelzer).**

ACES

NAME	SCORE	OTHER GROUPS
William H. Lewis	8.	
Darrell S. Cramer	7.5	347
Elwyn G. Righetti	7.5	
Earl R. Fryer	6.5	
Bernard H. Howes	6.	
Robert E. Welch	6.	
Dudley M. Amoss	5.5	
Robert L. Buttke	5.5	
William H. Allen	5.	
Gerald A. Brown	5.	4
Merle M. Coons	5.	
Russell C. Haworth	5.	
John L. McGinn	5.	
Thomas D. Schank	5.	
John D. Landers *	14.5	49/357/78

* Victories primarily with other units.

WILLIAM H. LEWIS (8.) - The native of Pasadena, California had the unique distinction of receiving credit for an enemy plane attacking him from the rear. On a mission in December 1944, Lewis was being pursued in a steep dive by a German fighter. Lewis pulled out but when the German tried to follow, his wing separated and he went in. His biggest day came on 5 September 1944 when he and three other pilots tangled with some sixteen planes and downed all of them. Lewis was credited with four of the victories. His planes were coded CY☆S. (Credit: W. Smelzer, W. Hess).

ELWYN G. RIGHETTI (7.5) - In addition to his aerial victories, Righetti scored 27 ground victories to lead the Eighth in that category. On 24 December 1944 he downed three FW-190s. Righetti rose to command the 55TH from February 1945 until he was lost on 17 April. On this date he had led the Group on a successful attack against German planes on the ground (he was credited with nine himself) when he bellied in. Righetti survived the crash only to be killed by hostile civilians a mere four days before the Group flew its last mission (Credit: W. Smelzer).

WILLIAM H. ALLEN (5.) - Like William Lewis, Allen's big day came on 5 September 1944. In fact all of his aerial victories came on this date when the flight led by Lewis ran into sixteen German planes and downed all of them (Credit: W. Hess).

ROBERT L. BUTTKE (5.5) - Buttke, a veteran of two tours with the 55TH, scored his half victory on 27 February 1945. On this occasion, he and Lloyd Boring teamed to down a Ju-88. His P-51 was named "Lovenia" and was coded CY☆F. This plane carried the pilot's name and those of his crew on the canopy frame (Credit: W. Smelzer).

P-38 - No markings

38th

338th

343rd

All (from Jul 44)

38th (from March 45)

338th (from Oct. 44)

343rd (from Oct. 44)

Dark green and yellow bands or spinner. Dark green & yellow checkerboard extending back 12 inches.

2 inch band in back of checkerboard on cowl in squadron color (from late 44).

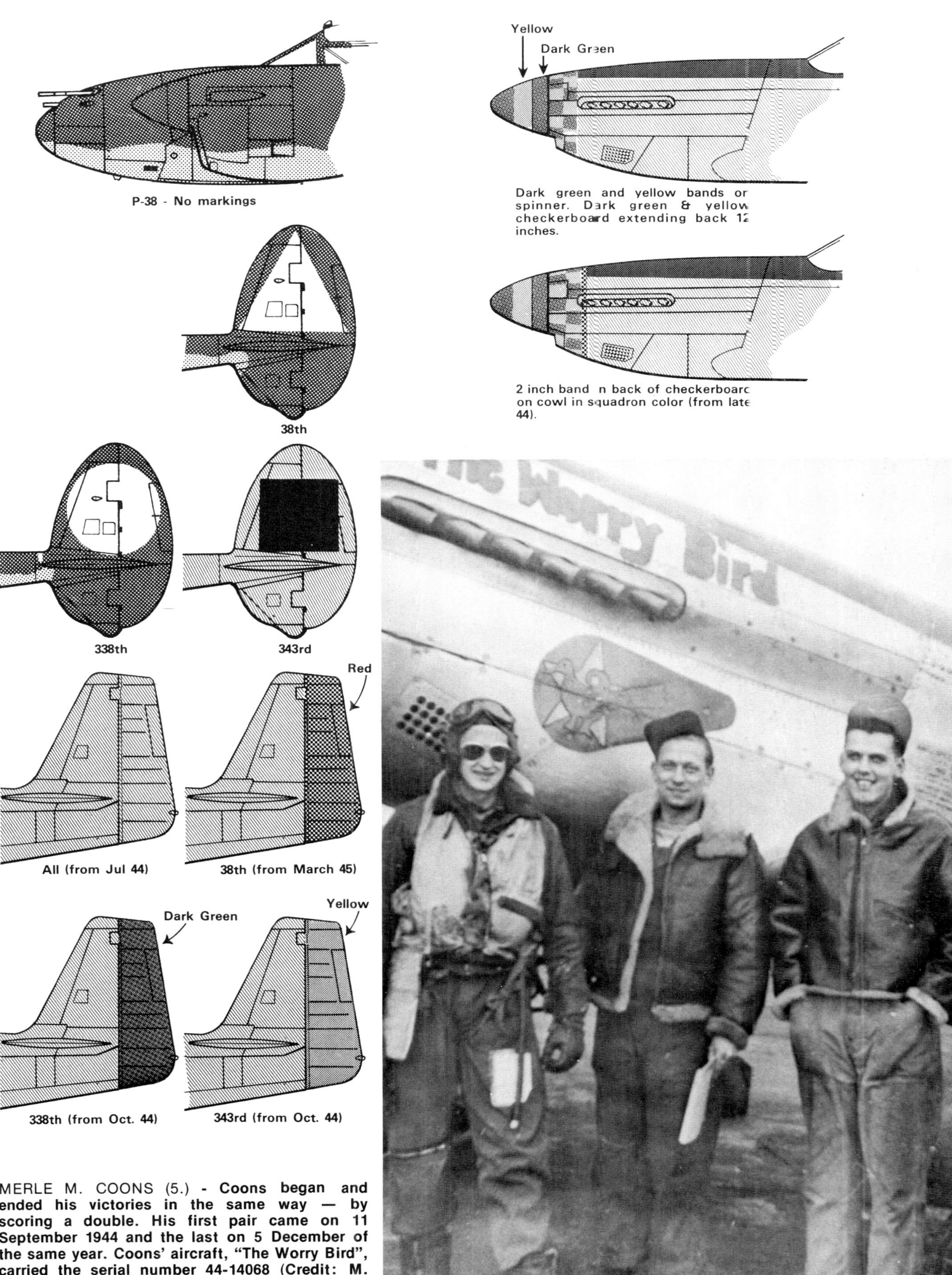

MERLE M. COONS (5.) - Coons began and ended his victories in the same way — by scoring a double. His first pair came on 11 September 1944 and the last on 5 December of the same year. Coons' aircraft, "The Worry Bird", carried the serial number 44-14068 (Credit: M. Coons).

56th Fighter Group

The **56TH Fighter Group** was activated on 15 January 1941 at Savannah AAB, Georgia. For the next eighteen months the unit moved to several bases on the East Coast and in June 1943 became the first group in the USAAF to take the new P-47 on strength. In January 1943 the Group headed overseas and settled into its first home, Kings Cliffe, on 13 January. Before flying its first combat mission, however, the Group moved to Horsham St. Faith. There were two more moves in store for the 56TH. The first of these was to Halesworth (8 July 1943) and the second to Boxted (18 April 1944). The 56TH was one of the highest scoring units in the USAAF. The 647½ aerial victories placed it on top in the Eighth Air Force in that category and it finished second only to the 4TH Fighter Group in combined air and ground victories. The outfit started into combat flying the P-47 and, unlike other Eighth outfits did not change to the Mustang. The Group finished the war flying the M-model of the Jug. The first Distinguished Unit Citation was awarded for the period of 20 February - 9 March 1944 when the Group destroyed 98 enemy planes. A second DUC was awarded for support provided to the airborne invasion of Holland on 18 September 1944. The 56TH flew its first combat mission on 13 April 1943 and by the end of hostilities had totaled 447 missions. 128 aircraft were lost by the Group and its eight to one kill-loss ratio was the best in the Eighth.

Squadron Codes ● 61st - **HV**, 62nd - **LM**, 63rd - **UN**

FRANCIS S. GABRESKI (28.) - **The native of Oil City, Pennsylvania was at Pearl Harbor when the war opened and served with 315 "Polish" Squadron before he joined the 56TH. He scored one triple and eight doubles while with the Group. Gabreski was commander of the 61ST Squadron when, on 20 July 1944, he was lost in action. Gabreski was strafing a German airfield when his prop struck the ground and he bellied in. He avoided capture for a few days but was eventually captured and spent the rest of the war as a guest of the Germans. All of Gabreski's aircraft were coded HV ☆ A and none carried any personal markings other than his victories. The photo above shows one of his earlier Thunderbolts (42-75510). His last plane was the bubble-top pictured on the right (42-26418). This plane was a mottled gray and green on the upper surfaces and was natural metal on the lower surfaces (Credit: D. Robinson, USAF).**

DAVID C. SCHILLING (22.5) - Schilling was born in Kansas but was raised in Michigan. He commanded the 62ND when the Group arrived in England and eventually rose to command the 56TH. His biggest day came on 23 December 1944 when he downed five enemy aircraft. Schilling also had one triple and three doubles to his credit. All of his planes were coded LM☆S (Credit: R.A. Johnson).

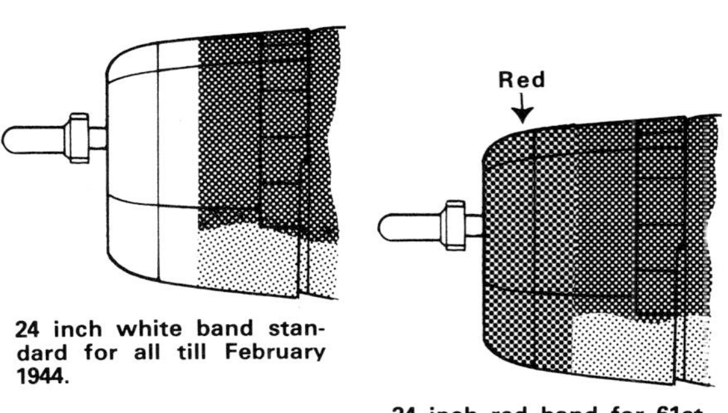

24 inch white band standard for all till February 1944.

24 inch red band for 61st squadron in Feb. and Mar. 1944.

ROBERT S. JOHNSON (28.) - The Lawton, Oklahoma native shared the honor of being top-gun in the ETO with Gabreski. Among his victories were one triple and seven doubles. Johnson was the first pilot in the ETO to break Eddie Rickenbacker's WW I record of 26 aerial victories. Though most of Johnson's kills were scored while he flew with the 61ST Squadron, he served for a period as the Operations Officer for the 62ND Squadron. Johnson flew five aircraft while with the 56TH and the first four of these were coded HV☆P. "Half Pint" was his first and the one in which he was almost shot down. His third aircraft, "Lucky" (42-8461), was his favorite but was lost in the North Sea by another pilot. His last ship was coded LM☆Q (42-25512) (Credit: R. Johnson).

FRED J. CHRISTENSEN, JR. (21.5) - Watertown, Massachusetts was his hometown and he was the only one of the top aces of the 56TH to join the Group after it had entered combat. Christensen was the first pilot in the Eighth to down six enemy planes on one mission (7 July 1944). The aircraft shown here was coded LM☆C (42-75207). His second plane was also LM☆C (42-26628) (Credit: W. Hess).

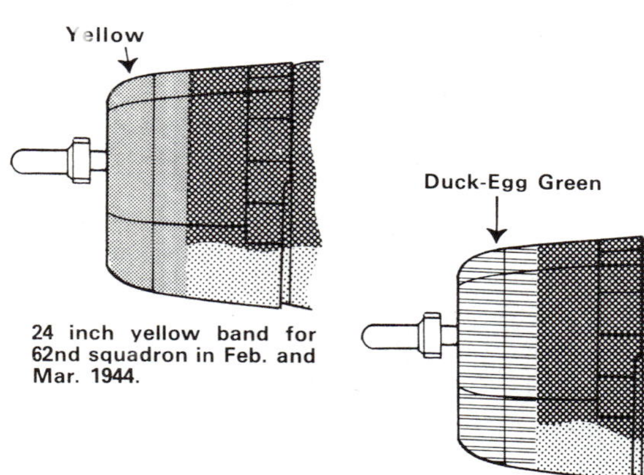

24 inch yellow band for 62nd squadron in Feb. and Mar. 1944.

24 inch duck-egg green band for 63rd squadron in Feb. and Mar. 1944.

WALKER M. MAHURIN (21.) - The Fort Wayne, Indiana native scored triples on three occasions and had three doubles to his credit. On 27 March 1944 he was shot down by the tail-gunner of his last victory. He evaded capture and eventually returned to England. He later served in the Pacific where he was credited with one Japanese bomber. His aircraft, shown on the back cover, was his personal mount for nearly his entire tour with the 56TH (Credit: W. Mahurin).

GERALD W. JOHNSON (17.) - Johnson hailed from Owenton, Kentucky. He served for a brief period with the 356TH Fighter Group and on his return to the 56TH took command of the 63RD Squadron. Johnson went down on 27 March 1944 and was made a POW. His aircraft, HV ☆ D (42-7877), was named "In The Mood". The presentation message on the port side read "Jackson County, Michigan, Fighter". With the 63RD his aircraft was UN ☆ V (42-76249) (Credit: D. Morris).

HUBERT A. ZEMKE (17.75) - His hometown was Missoula, Montana and he was the original combat commander of the 56TH. Zemke served two tours in this capacity. He gave up the position in August 1944. Rated as one of the best wartime commanders, Zemke took command of the 479TH after he left the 56TH. He went down due to engine trouble on 30 October 1944 and was made a POW. The plane shown here was coded UN ☆ Z (41-6330) (Credit: D. Smith).

ACES

NAME	SCORE	OTHER GROUPS
Francis S. Gabreski	28.	
Robert S. Johnson	28.	
David C. Schilling	22.5	
Frederick J. Christensen, Jr.	21.5	
Walker M. Mahurin	21.	3AC
Hubert A. Zemke	17.75	479
Gerald R. Johnson	17.	356
Joseph H. Powers	14.5	
Felix D. Williamson	13.	
James C. Stewart	12.5	
Michael G. Quirk	12.	
Leroy A. Schreiber	12.	
Paul A. Conger	11.5	
Robert J. Rankin	10.	
George E. Bostwick	9.	
Stanley B. Morrill	9.	
Billy C. Edens	8.	
Michael J. Jackson	8.	
Glenn D. Schiltz	8.	
John W. Vogt, Jr.	8.	356
Frank W. Klibbe	7.	
Robert A. Lamb	7.	
Leslie C. Smith	7.	
John H. Truluck	7.	
Joseph H. Bennett	6.5	4
Mark L. Mosely	6.5	
James R. Carter	6.	
Walter V. Cook	6.	
George F. Hall	6.	
Cameron M. Hart	6.	
Robert J. Keen	6.	
Frank E. McCauley	5.5	
Donovan F. Smith	5.5	
Harold E. Comstock	5.	
Lucien C. Dade, Jr.	5.	
Joseph L. Egan, Jr.	5.	
Steven N. Gerick	5.	
Norman D. Gould	5.	
Joseph W. Icard	5.	
Evan D. McMinn	5.	
Eugene W. O'Neill, Jr.	5.	

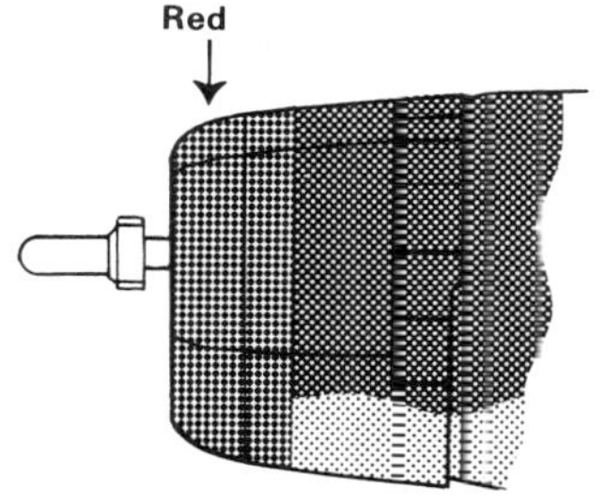

24 inch red band for all group planes after March 1944.

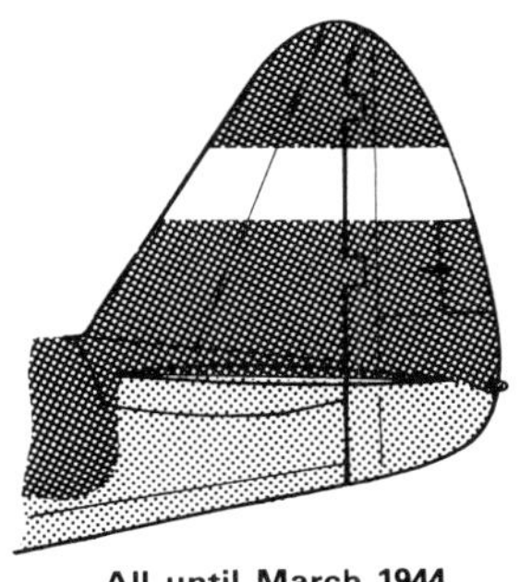

All until March 1944

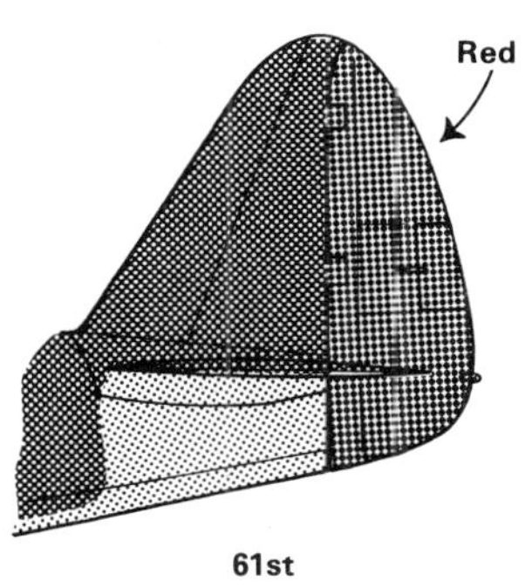

61st

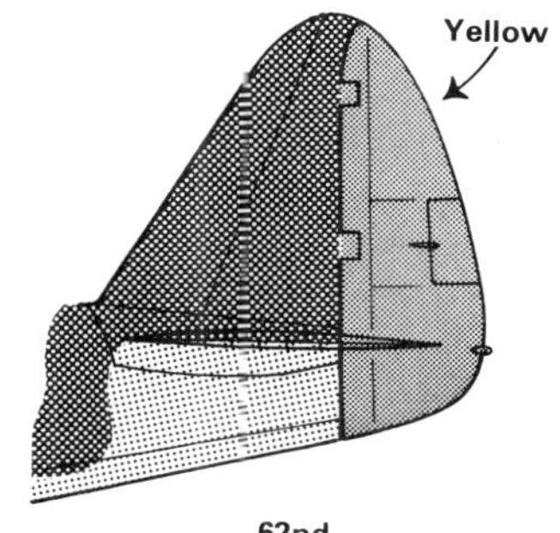

62nd

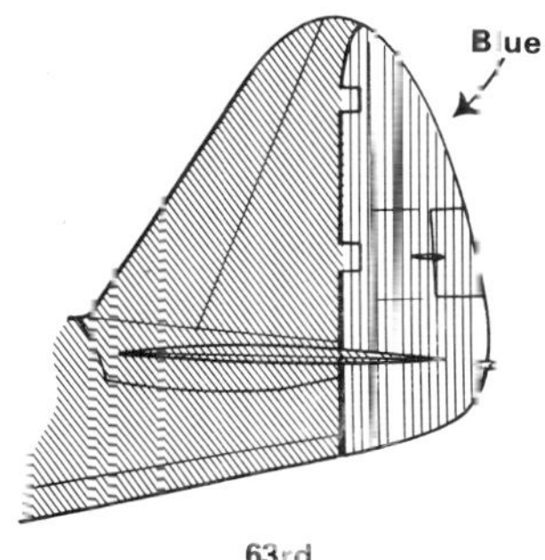

63rd

78th Fighter Group

The **78TH Fighter Group** was activated on 9 February 1942 and did most of its initial training at March Field, California. The unit was selected to be one of the first outfits to equip with the P-38. It was with this aircraft that the 78TH shipped out for England in November 1942. It settled into its first home, Goxhill, on 1 December 1943, but the Group moved to its permanent home, Duxford, just prior to its first combat mission on 13 April 1943. Being one of the first three fighter groups to be permanently assigned to the Eighth Air Force meant that the 78TH was in the thick of things from the beginning. Among the firsts established were the first ace (Charles London), the first triple (Eugene Roberts), and the first ground strafing by a P-47 pilot (Quince Brown). Although the Group flew the P-38 when it first arrived in England, it converted to the P-47 in February 1943. The Thunderbolt was standard equipment until the end of 1944. At that time the conversion to the P-51 began and by January 1945 the 78TH was mounted completely in the Mustang. Two Distinguished Unit Citations were presented to the outfit for its actions. The first of these was for support of the airborne invasion of Holland (16-23 September 1944). The second was for ground strafing of enemy aircraft on 16 April 1945. On this mission the 78TH established an Eighth Air Force record by destroying 135 German planes. In 450 combat missions, the 78TH destroyed 338½ enemy planes in the air and 358½ on the ground for a loss of 167 of its own aircraft.

Squadron Codes ● 82nd - **MX**, 83rd - **HL**, 84th - **WZ**

ALDWIN M. JUCHEIM (10.) - **When the month of April 1944 opened, the Grenada, Mississippi native was a 2nd Lieutenant but during the month he tallied three doubles and was up for Captain. On one occasion he literally rode an FW-190 into the ground when he was out of ammo. His aircraft was coded HL ☆J (42-26020) (Credit: USAF).**

QUINCE L. BROWN (12.34) - Quince Brown was a native of Bristow, Oklahoma. On 20 July 1943 he was returning from a mission on the deck and, when an enemy locomotive and a gun emplacement presented themselves, he became the first pilot in the ETO to use the Thunderbolt for strafing. While on another strafing mission almost a year later, he was hit by ground fire and bellied in. He made the landing in good shape but he was captured by German civilians and killed by them. Brown's first P-47, "Okie" was coded WZ☆J (42-74573). His later P-47 was also coded WZ☆J and may have received some personal markings at a later date (Credit: USAF).

JOHN D. LANDERS (14.5) - Landers' first tour of duty was in the Pacific with the 49TH Fighter Group where he scored six of his victories. After a brief stay in the States he was assigned to the Eighth Air Force and served with several of the groups beginning with the 55TH. After this, he commanded the 357TH for a short time and then the 78TH. After the war he also commanded the 361ST Fighter Group. In addition to his 8½ aerial victories with the Eighth Air Force, he was credited with 20 enemy planes destroyed on the ground including eight on one mission. His aircraft while with the 78TH was named "Big Beautiful Doll" and was coded WZ☆I (44-72258) (Credit: J. Landers).

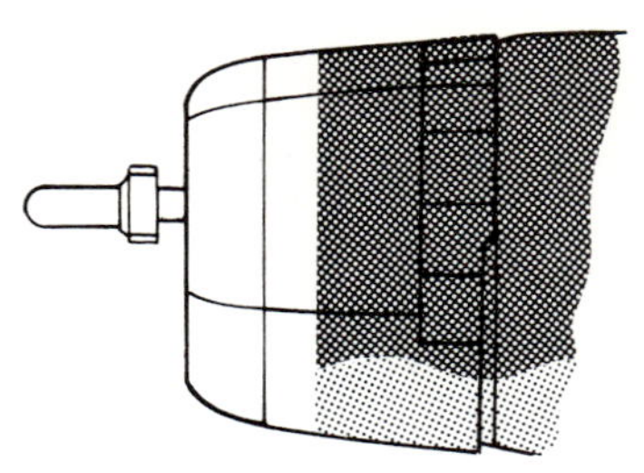

24 inch white band standard on all aircraft until April 1944.

EUGENE P. ROBERTS (9.) - Roberts' hometown was Spokane, Washington. He scored the first triple in the Eighth Air Force on 30 July 1943 and became one of the first aces in the ETO. He also served with the 364TH Fighter Group as its commander from January to November 1945. His aircraft was WZ☆Z (41-6330) and was named after his hometown (Credit: D. Glover).

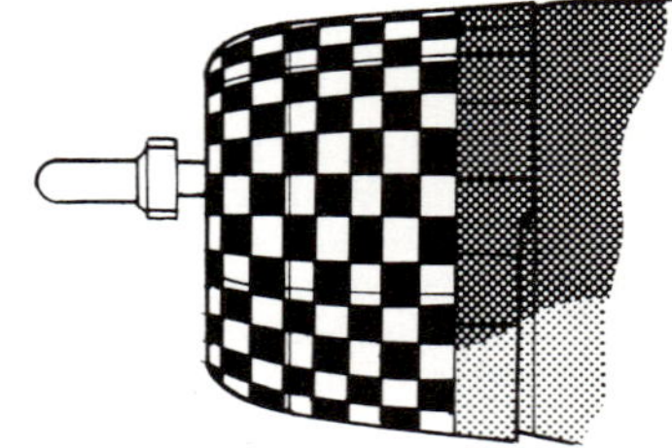

Black and white checkerboard extending to cowl shutters from April 1944.

PETER G. POMPETTI (5.5) - Pompetti was one of the early aces of the Eighth Air Force. The Philadelphian scored a double on the "Ramrod to Emden" mission of 27 September 1943. Pompetti was eventually lost in action (17 March 1944) and made a prisoner by the Germans. His aircraft, "Axe the Axis" was coded WZ☆R (41-6393) (Credit: P. Pompetti).

CHARLES P. LONDON (5.) - London, a native of Long Beach, California, was a flight leader with the 83RD Squadron. He scored his first victory on 22 June 1943 and added a double on the 29th of the same month. On 30 July he downed an FW-190 and an Me-109 to become the first ace in the Eighth. His aircraft was coded HL ☆ B (41-6335) and was named "El Jeepo" (Credit: USAF, C. London).

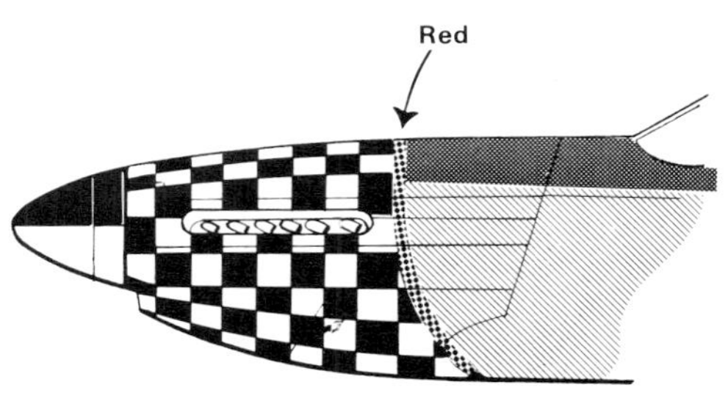

Black and white checkerboard used on all P-51s. This was usually outlined with a red band.

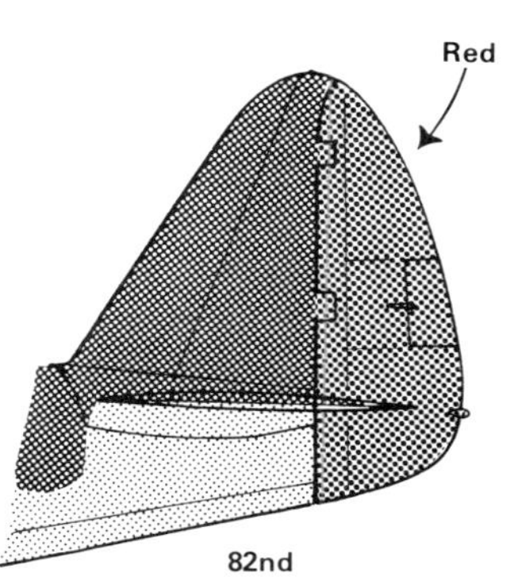

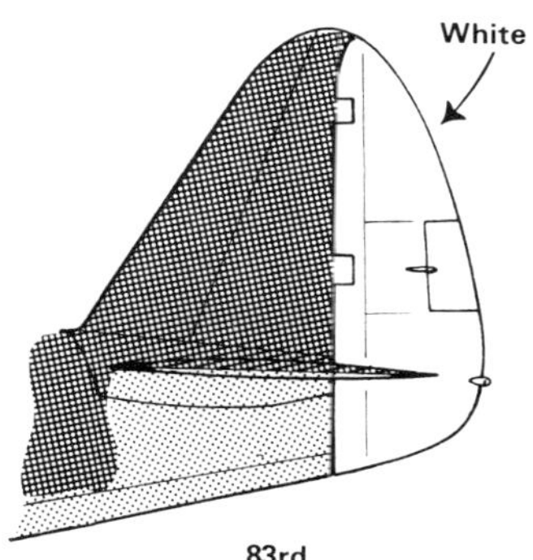

ACES

NAME	SCORE	OTHER GROUPS
Quince L. Brown	12.34	
Aldwin M. Jucheim	10.	
Eugene P. Roberts, Jr.	9.	364
John D. Landers *	14.5	49/357/55
John J. Hockery	7.	
James W. Wilkinson	7.	
Grant M. Turley	6.	
Warren H. Wesson	6.	
Peter G. Pompetti	5.5	
Robert R. Bonebrake	5.	
William H. Julian	5.	
Charles P. London	5.	
Ben I. Mayo	5.	
Jack G. Oberhansly	5	4
Jack C. Price	5	20

* 8 5 victories with 8TH AF

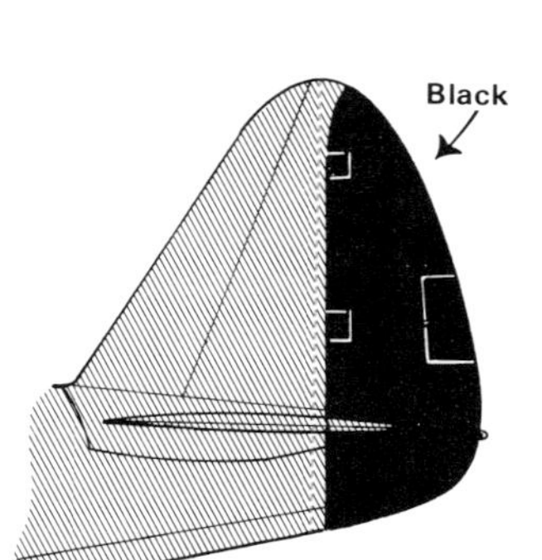

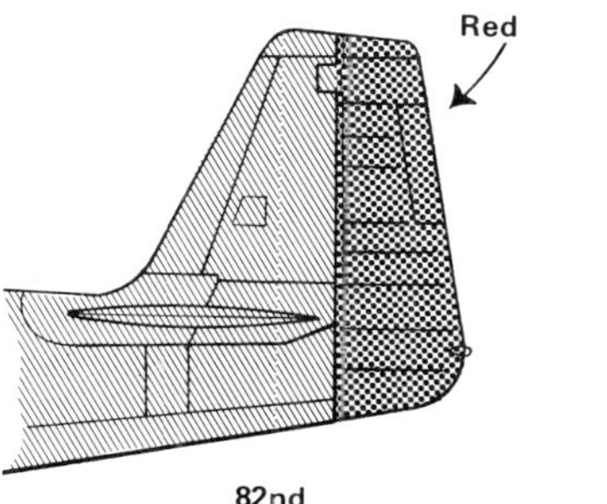

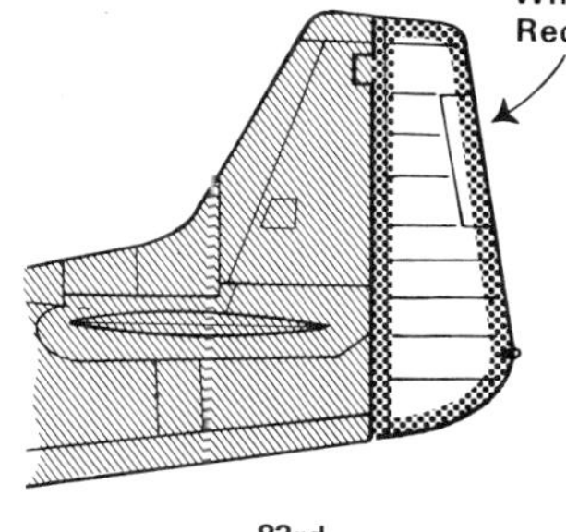

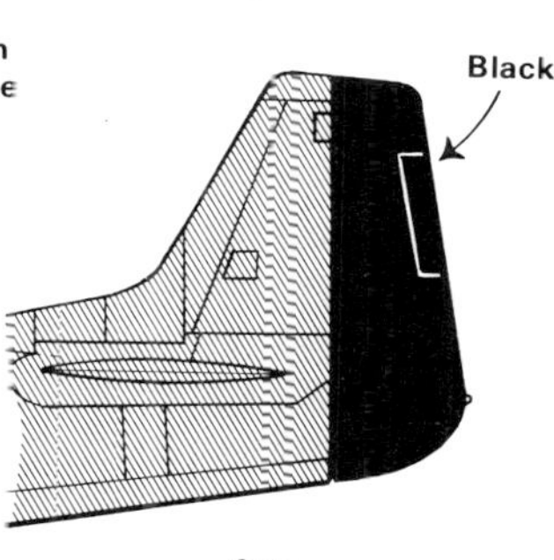

SQUADRON TAIL COLORS INTRODUCED NOVEMBER 1944

339th Fighter Group

The **339TH Fighter Group** was established as the **339TH Bomb Group** at Hunter Field, Georgia on 10 August 1942. Originally equipped with A-24 and A-25s and trained in the dive-bombing role, the unit was redesignated as a Fighter-Bomber Group on 15 August 1943. The 339TH sailed for Europe still with this designation and established its base at Fowlmere on 5 April 1944. The Group flew its first combat mission on 30 April 1944 but it was not until May of that year that it was officially designated as the **339TH Fighter Group.** In the States the outfit had been working up on P-39s but on arrival in England, it was assigned Mustangs. As a result the Group entered combat with little experience in the plane it was to fly for the rest of the war. The outfit was awarded the Distinguished Unit Citation for the period of 10 and 11 September 1944. In this two day period it destroyed 58 enemy planes while on escort duties. The Group flew 264 missions and destroyed a total of 239½ German aircraft in the air and 440½ on the ground (second highest in the Eighth) for a loss of 97 airplanes. The 339TH was the only group to claim over 100 victories on the ground on two occasions (105 on 4 April and 118 on 11 April 1945) and its total ground and air victories during its one year of combat set a record for the Eighth.

Squadron Codes ● 503rd - **D7**, 504th - **6N**, 505th - **5Q**

FRANCIS R. GERARD (8.) - **The Lyndhurst, New Jersey native served two tours of duty with the 339TH and amassed a total of 420 combat hours. His biggest day came on 11 September 1944 when he tied into a large group of Germans over Leipzig. When the smoke had cleared, Gerard had downed four of the enemy planes in just twelve minutes. He also scored a double on 2 March 1945. (Credit: F. Gerard).**

(Below right) JAMES R. STARNES (6.) - **Starnes scored well in the air and on the ground. By the end of the war he had 6½ German planes to his credit by strafing. The Wilmington, North Carolina native may well have been the first Eighth Air Force pilot to do his strafing in Czechoslovakia. This came on a mission in early February 1945.**

(Below) ROBERT H. AMMON (5.) - **In addition to his score in the air, Ammon destroyed nine German planes on the ground. All of these were scored on a single mission on 16 April 1945. His victories in the air were all over FW-190s and included two doubles. The twin kills came on 23 and 28 September 1944. Ammon named his plane "Annie May" and it carried the codes 5Q☆U.**

EVAN M. JOHNSON (5.) - All together Johnson contributed to the destruction of eight German planes in the air of which six were shared with other pilots. On 24 May 1944 he was pursuing a German plane in a near vertical dive. Johnson was finally able to pull out of the dive quite close to the ground but in doing so his wings buckled. The German was not as lucky — he crashed (Credit: USAF).

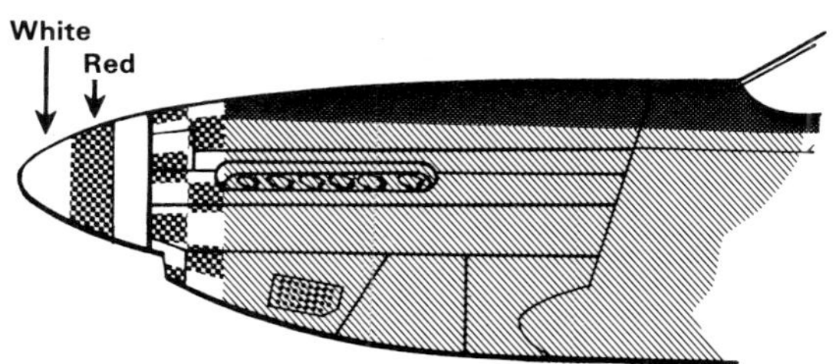

Red & white bands on spinner. 12 inch checkerboard band on front of cowl in red & white.

JOSEPH THURY (2.5) - **Thury was the second highest ground scorer in the Eighth Air Force with 25½ planes to his credit. His highest one day total came on 17 April 1945 when he destroyed five German planes. On two other occasions, he destroyed four planes and he had multiple victories on several other missions. Thury's "Pauline" was coded 6N☆C and carried the serial 44-14656 (Credit: USAF).**

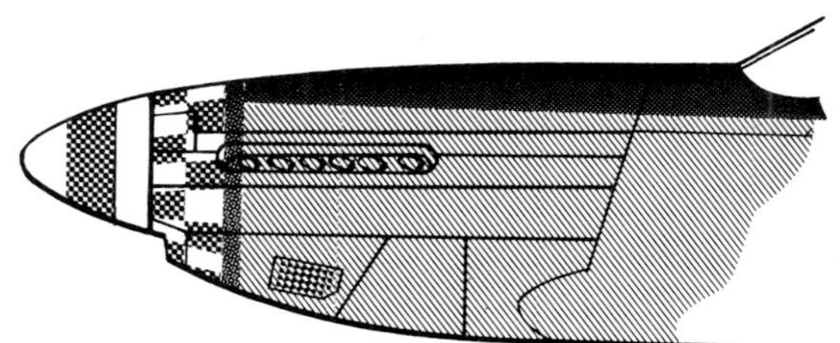

Thin band behind checkerboard cowl band in squadron color (from early 45).

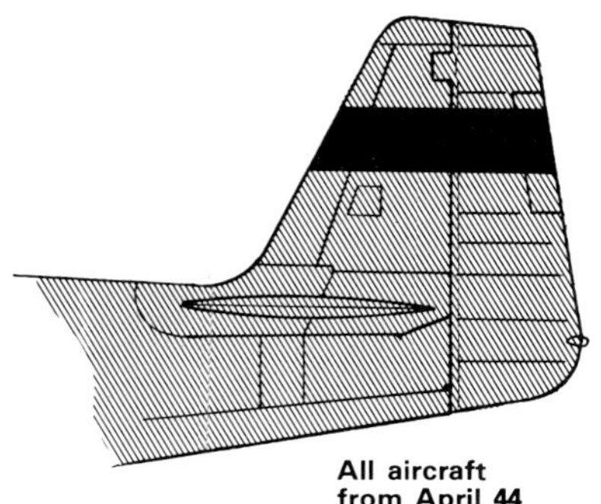

All aircraft from April 44

KIRKE B. EVERSON (1.5) - **In addition to his aerial victories, Everson scored thirteen ground victories. This total was enough to give him the lead in this category for the 504TH Squadron. Everson scored over half of his ground victories on 17 April when he was credited with seven German planes. His shared air victory, over an Me-262, came on 3 April (Credit: USAF).**

WILLIAM C. CLARK (1.) - Clark, the last wartime commander of the 339TH took command of the Group on 14 April 1945. In addition to his one aerial kill, he scored eight ground victories. Six of these came on 16 April 1945 during strafing attacks on four German airfields. His aircraft, "Happy IV", was coded 5Q☆C (44-64148) and is shown in a color photo on the back cover (Credit: W. Clark).

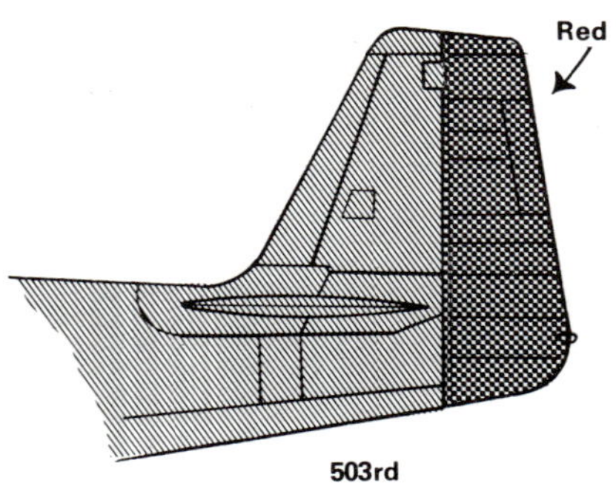

ACES

NAME	SCORE	OTHER GROUPS
William E. Bryan, Jr.	8.5	
Francis R. Gerard	8.	
Dale E. Schafer, Jr.	8.	31
Donald A. Larson	6.	
James R. Starnes	6.	
Robert H. Ammon	5.	
Edward H. Beavers, Jr.	5.	
J.S. Daniel	5.	
Christopher J. Hanseman	5.	
Evan M. Johnson	5.	
Lester C. Marsh	5.	
Michael G.H. McPharlin *	5.5	RAF/4

* Victories primarily with other units.

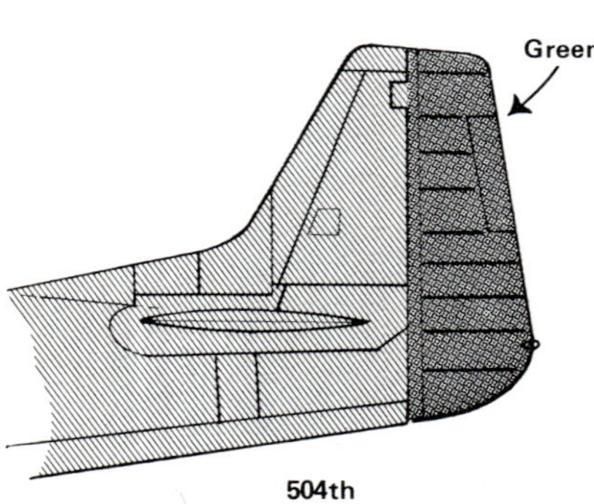

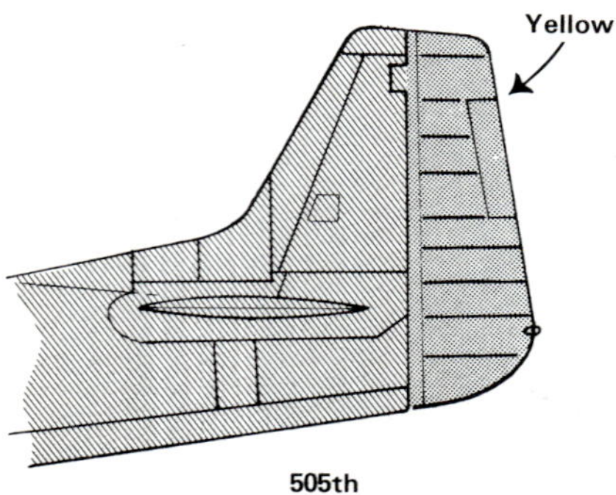

SQUADRON TAIL MARKINGS
(from November 1944)

JOHN B. HENRY, JR. (0) - Henry did not have any confirmed victories either in the air or on the ground. He did, however, receive credit for probably destroying an Me-262 on 30 March 1945. Henry was the first commander of the 339TH and served in that capacity until 13 April 1945 (Credit: USAF).

352nd Fighter Group

The **352ND Fighter Group** was activated on 1 October 1942 at Mitchell Field, Long Island with two of its squadrons, the 486TH and 487TH, being redesignations of squadrons that had seen action in the Pacific. The unit began to train on the P-47 in March 1943 and in July of that year set sail for England. Upon arrival, the Group took up residence at Bodney on 8 July. The 352ND operated from this base until late December 1944 when the air echelons transferred to the Continent. The Group operated from Asche and then Chievres until April 1945 at which time it returned to Bodney. The 487TH Squadron became the only squadron in the Eighth to be independently awarded the Distinguished Unit Citation for its efforts on 1 January 1945. On this date the Squadron destroyed 23 enemy aircraft. The Group was also awarded a DUC for its support of a bombing mission to Brunswick on 8 May 1944. The 352ND flew the P-47 from its entry into combat on 9 September 1943 until the latter part of April 1944. At that time, the Group began conversion to the Mustang. Through the remainder of the war the outfit operated the P-51 including the B, C, D, and K models. On 2 November 1944 the group shot down 38 German planes to register the second highest single day score. The Group flew 420 combat missions and destroyed 519½ German planes in the air. Another 287 were destroyed on the ground. Combat losses for the 352ND were 118 aircraft.

Squadron Codes ● 328th - **PE**, 486th - **PZ**, 487th - **HO**

GEORGE E. PREDDY (25.83) - **The highest scoring ace in a Mustang, Preddy was from Greensboro, North Carolina. He served in the Pacific before joining the 352ND and had claims for two Japanese planes damaged. He flew two tours with the 352ND and eventually commanded the 328TH Squadron. Preddy's biggest day came on 6 August 1944 when he downed five enemy aircraft. His career ended tragically on Christmas 1944. While chasing a German low over the American lines the American troops opened fire and Preddy was killed. His aircraft were all named "Cripes A'Mighty" and his individual aircraft number was "P" except for one which was coded "P" when with the 487TH. (Credit: W. Smelzer).**

ACES

NAME	SCORE	OTHER GROUPS
George E. Preddy	25.83	
John C. Meyer	24.	
John F. Thornell	17.25	
William T. Whisner	16.	
Donald S. Bryan	13.34	
Glennon T. Moran	13.	
William T. Halton	11.5	
Raymond H. Littge	10.5	
Stephen W. Andrew	9.	49
Virgil K. Merony	9.	
Charles J. Cesky	8.5	
Frank A. Cutler	8.5	
Carl J. Luksic	8.5	
Sanford K. Moats	8.5	
Henry J. Miklajyck	7.5	
Willie O. Jackson	7.	
Walter E. Starck	6.	
Edwin L. Heller	5.5	
Francis W. Horne	5.5	
Ernest O. Bostrom	5.	
Clayton E. Davis	5.	
Earl R. Lazear	5.	
Joseph L. Mason	5.	
Duerr H. Schuh	5.	
Alexander F. Sears	5.	
William J. Stangel	5.	
Everett W. Stewart *	7.83	355/4
* Victories primarily with other units.		

JOHN C. MEYER (24.) - Meyer's hometown was Forrest Hills, New York. He joined the 352ND before it shipped out for England and when it did he went as commander of the 487TH Squadron. Meyer scored the first victory in the 352ND when he blasted an Me-109 from the sky on 26 November 1943. He scored a triple on two missions. On another mission he was credited with 2½ victories and he added doubles on three other occasions. All of Meyer's aircraft were coded HO☆M. His first, a P-47, was named "Lambie". Both of his Mustangs were named "Petie". The first of these (42-106471) was lost by another pilot on D-Day (Credit: USAF).

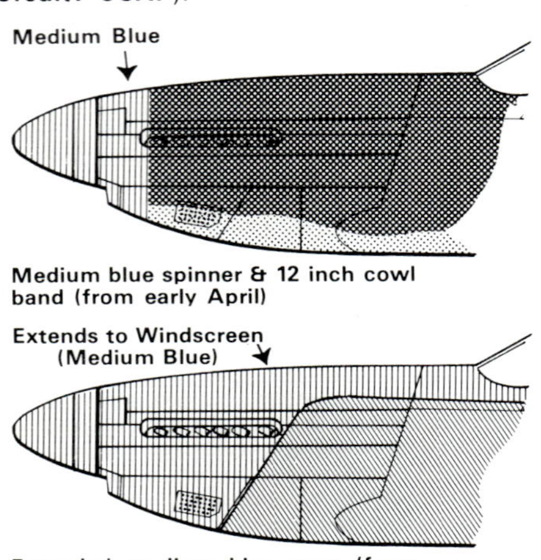

(Below right) DONALD S. BRYAN (13.34) - Bryan's score grew steadily through 1944 and was climaxed by five victories on 2 November 1944. On this escort mission to Merseberg he also damaged two other German fighters. His last victory, an Arado 234, came on 14 March 1945 just before he departed for his Paicines, California home. His "Little One III" was coded PE☆B (Credit: D. Bryan).

(Below) WILLIAM T. WHISNER (16) - This native of Shreveport, Louisiana flew 137 combat missions during his two tours with the 352ND. His biggest day came on 21 November 1944 when he downed five FW-190s. Whisner added another four German planes to his total on 5 January 1945. The name carried on this aircraft was "Moonbeam McSwine".

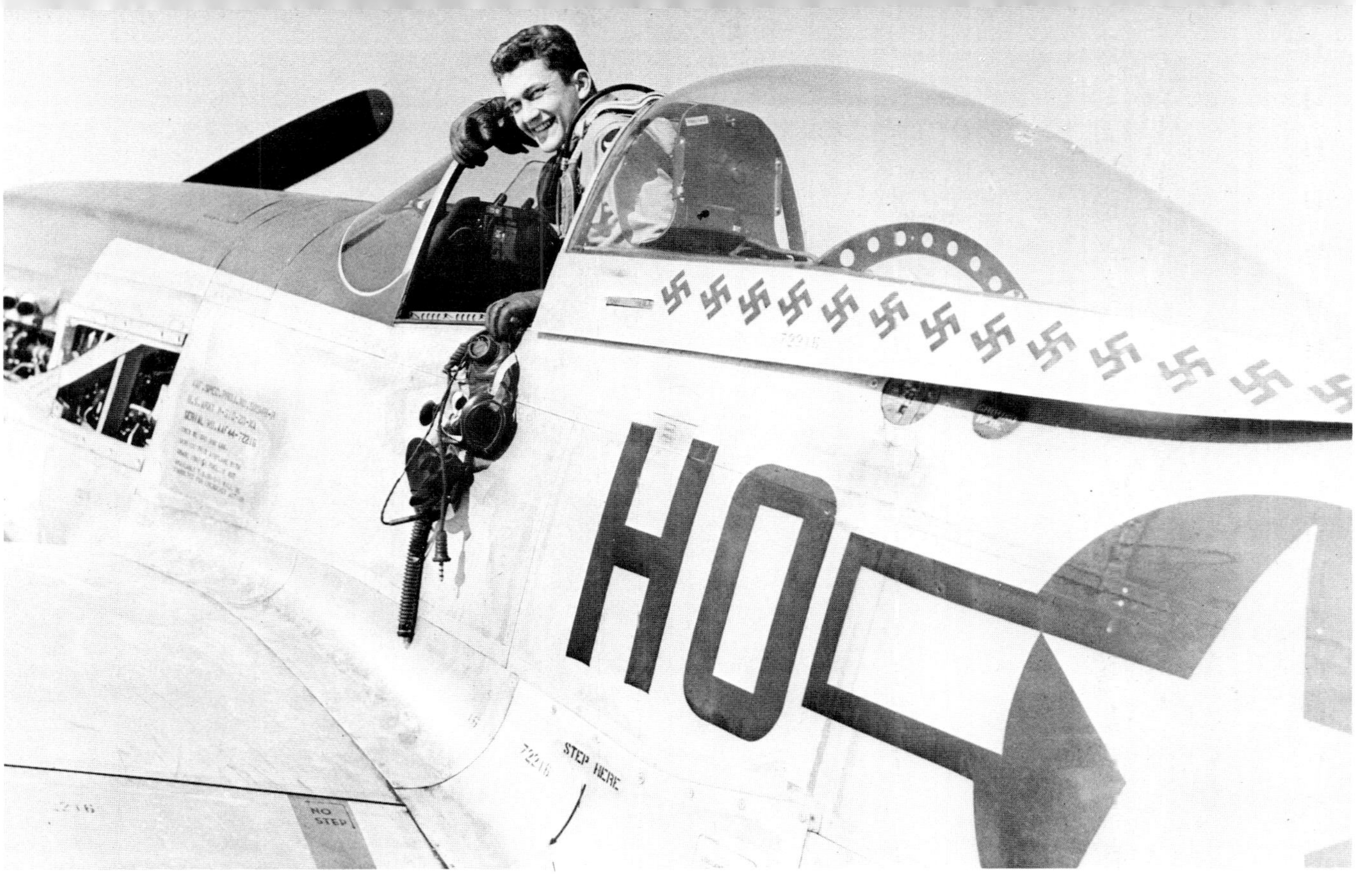

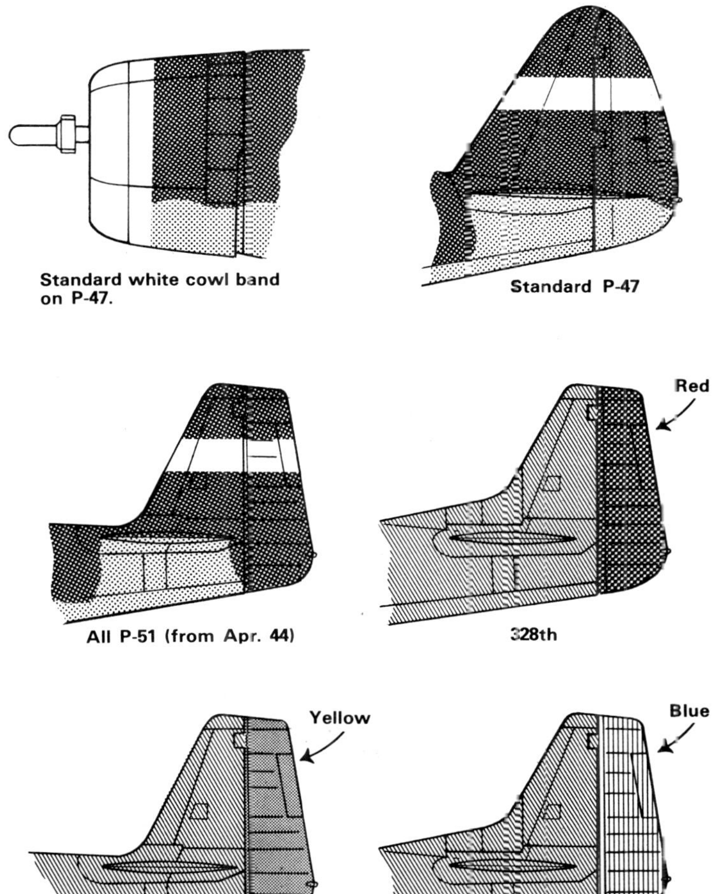

RAYMOND H. LITTGE (10.5) - **Littge was a native of Altenburg, Missouri. On one two-mission spree he destroyed a total of five enemy planes on the ground. The only information on his aircraft is the serial number (44-72216) (Credit: USAF).**

JOHN F. THORNELL (17.25) - **Thornell's hometown was East Walpole, Massachusetts. All of his victories were amassed during the first six months of 1944. Among his victories was a triple on 8 May 1944. His aircraft was named "Pattie Ann" and was coded PE☆T (42-106872).**

Standard white cowl band on P-47.

Standard P-47

All P-51 (from Apr. 44)

328th

486th

487th

SQUADRON TAIL COLORS (from November 44)

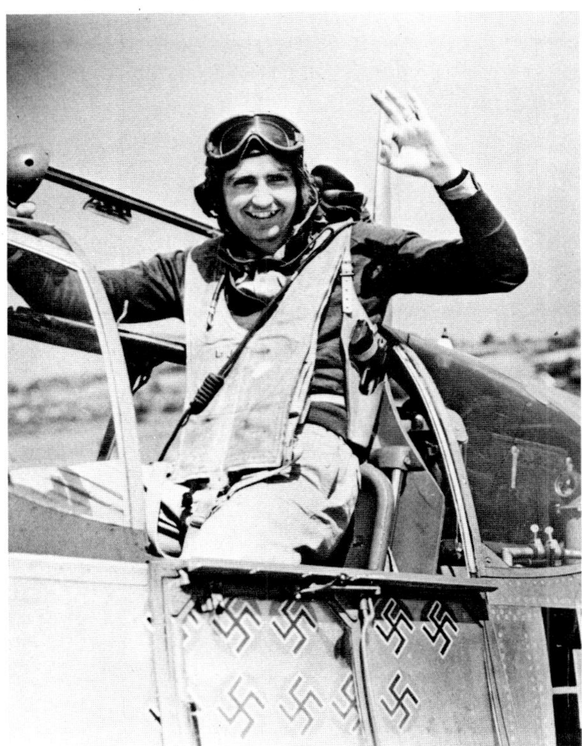

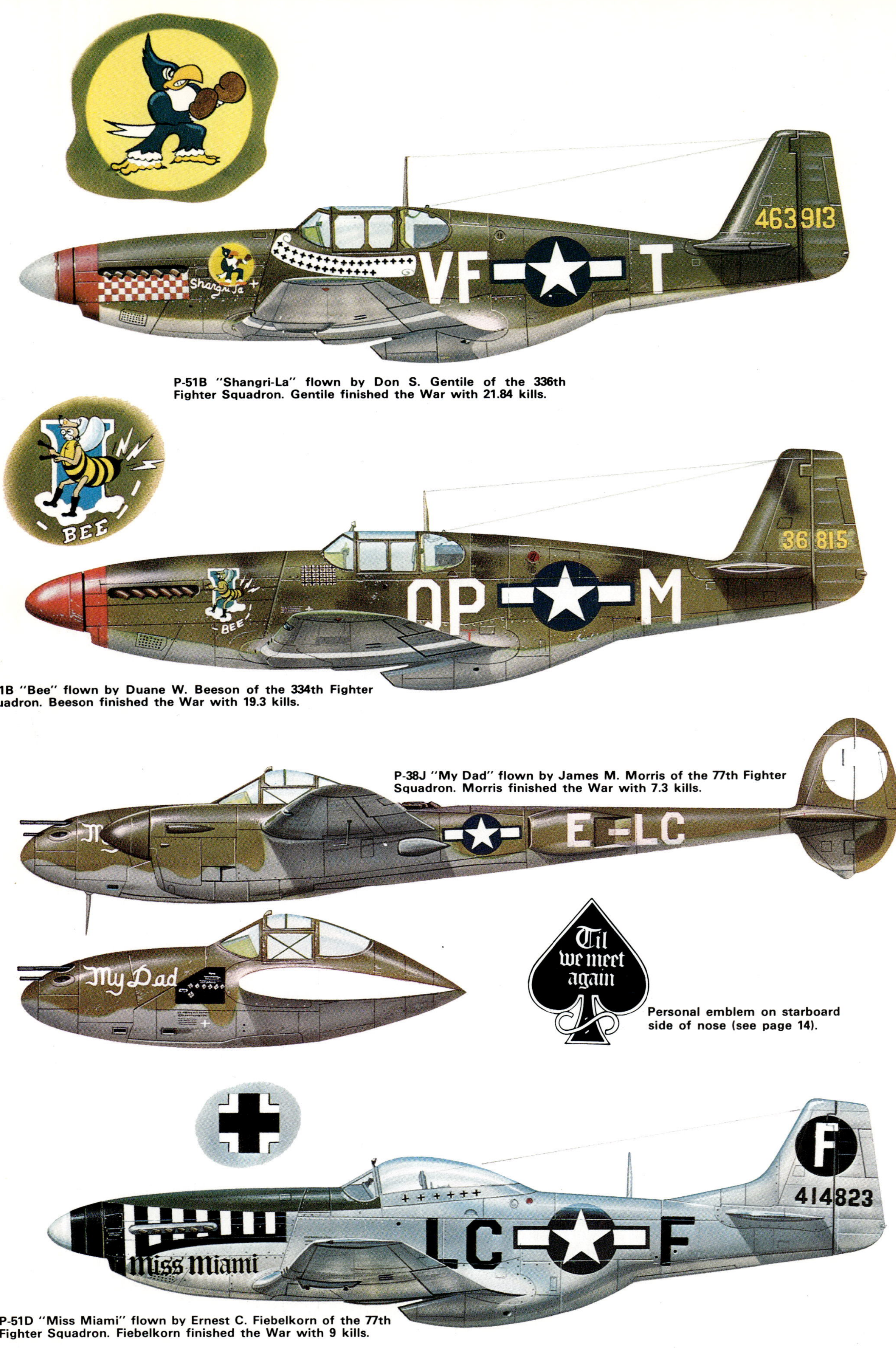

P-51B "Shangri-La" flown by Don S. Gentile of the 336th Fighter Squadron. Gentile finished the War with 21.84 kills.

P-51B "Bee" flown by Duane W. Beeson of the 334th Fighter Squadron. Beeson finished the War with 19.3 kills.

P-38J "My Dad" flown by James M. Morris of the 77th Fighter Squadron. Morris finished the War with 7.3 kills.

Personal emblem on starboard side of nose (see page 14).

P-51D "Miss Miami" flown by Ernest C. Fiebelkorn of the 77th Fighter Squadron. Fiebelkorn finished the War with 9 kills.

353rd Fighter Group

The **353RD Fighter Group** was activated at Mitchell Field, Long Island on 1 October 1942 but actual operations were centered at Baltimore, Maryland. The Group began to receive P-47s in February 1943 and in May of that year it was alerted for assignment to England. The first base for the unit overseas was Goxhill but the stay here was a short one (7 June - 3 August 1943). The Group moved to Metfield where it remained until April 1945. At that time it moved again, to Raydon, and stayed in this third location for the remainder of its stay in England. The first all 353RD combat mission was flown on 12 August 1943, but the first official mission for the Group took place on 9 August. Sixteen planes flew as a fourth squadron to the 56TH Fighter Group. The Group pioneered the dive-bombing and ground attack techniques later adopted as standard for the Eighth and Ninth Air Forces. The Group received one Distinguished Unit Citation for its efforts in support of the airborne invasion of Holland in September 1944. Original combat equipment for the unit was the Thunderbolt and it continued to use this plane until November 1944. The Group began the transition to the P-51 in October and continued to operate with this type until the end of the war. During 447 combat missions the 353RD scored 330½ aerial victories and an additional 414 on the ground. Losses for the Group totaled 137 aircraft.

Squadron Codes ● 350th - **LH**, 351st - **YJ**, 352nd - **SX**

ACES

NAME	SCORE	OTHER GROUPS
Glenn E. Duncan	19.	
Walter C. Beckham	18.	
Wayne K. Blickenstaff	10.	
Kenneth W. Gallup	9.	
William J. Maguire	7.	
James N. Poindexter	7.	
Gordon B. Compton	6.5	
William F. Tanner	5.5	
Robert W. Abernathy	5.	
Arthur C. Cundy	5.	
Robert A. Elder	5.	
Raymond E. Hartley	5.	325
Harrison B. Tordoff	5.	
Horace Q. Waggoner	5.	

GLENN E. DUNCAN (19.) - Duncan, a native of Houston, Texas, commanded the 353RD for the first time beginning in November 1943. On 7 July 1944 he was shot down by flak but evaded capture and eventually made contact with the Dutch underground. He worked with this organization until liberated by advancing Allied forces and returned to England where he resumed command of the 353RD on 22 April 1945. All of his victories were scored in Thunderbolts and, along with two other 353RD pilots scored the first ground victory in the Eighth Air Force. All of his planes were named "Dove of Peace" and coded LH☆X. Duncan's last plane, a P-51, carried the serial number 44-73060 (Credit: W. Smelzer).

WAYNE K. BLICKENSTAFF (10.) - Although Blickenstaff was one of the early members of the Group, he had to wait a long time for his first victory. When he finally scored, he did it in a big way by downing four Germans on 27 November 1944. Five more of his victories came on 24 March 1945. The name carried on his LH☆U was "Betty-E" (Credit: W. Blickenstaff).

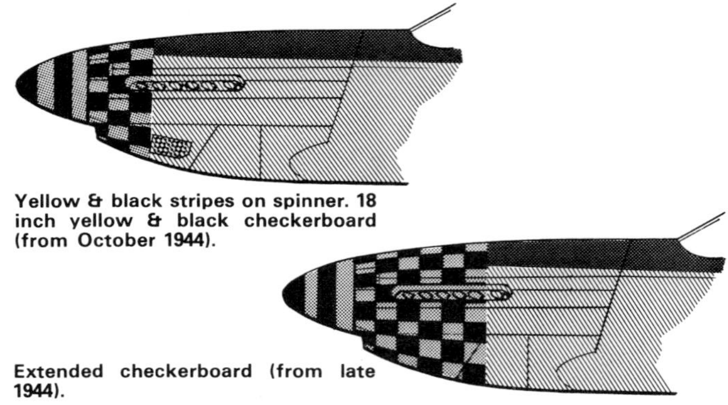

Yellow & black stripes on spinner. 18 inch yellow & black checkerboard (from October 1944).

Extended checkerboard (from late 1944).

WALTER C. BECKHAM (18.) - The De Funiak Springs, Florida native ran up an impressive string of victories in a five month period. His first victory came on 23 September 1943 and he scored a triple on 10 October of the same year. Beckham rose to command the 351ST Squadron. On 22 February 1944, he was hit by flak while on a strafing pass and bailed out. He was taken prisoner and at the time of his capture was the leading ace in the ETO. Beckham flew his "Little Demon" when he got most of his victories (Credit: USAF).

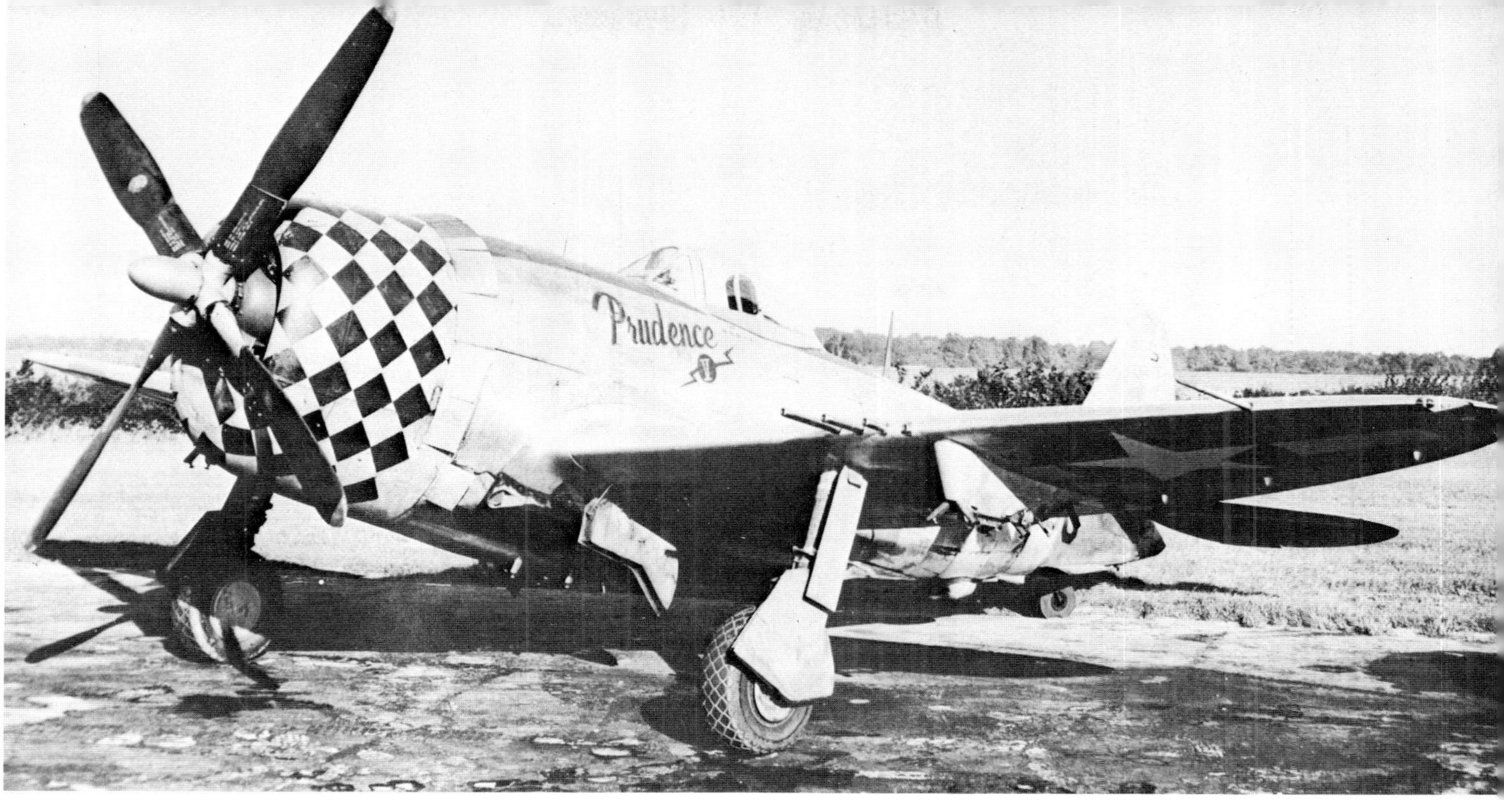

WILLIAM F. TANNER (5.5) - **Bill Tanner, a native of Canastota, New York, was one of the early scorers of the 353RD and he stayed with the Group after the war. His biggest day came over Steinhuder Lake, Germany on 5 December 1944 when he destroyed three FW-190s and damaged another. Tanner's aircraft was coded LH☆O (42-26472) (Credit: W. Tanner).**

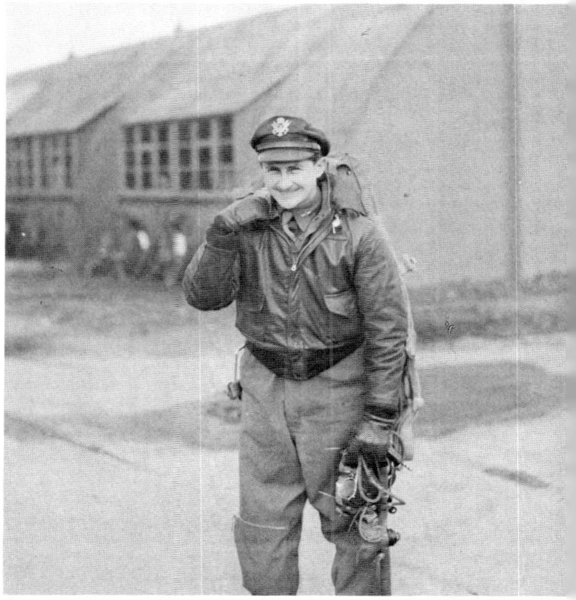

JAMES N. POINDEXTER (7.) - **Poindexter did his initial scoring in late 1943. His best scoring days came on 22 February and 30 May 1944 when he scored doubles. The flyer from Milville, New Jersey liked to close to point blank range in battle and on one occasion was able to record the German's markings on his combat report. Poindexter flew SX☆G ("Honey II") (Credit: D. Robinson).**

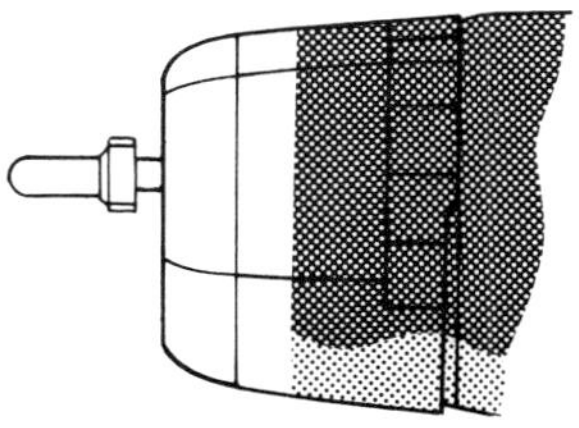

Standard white band until April 1944.

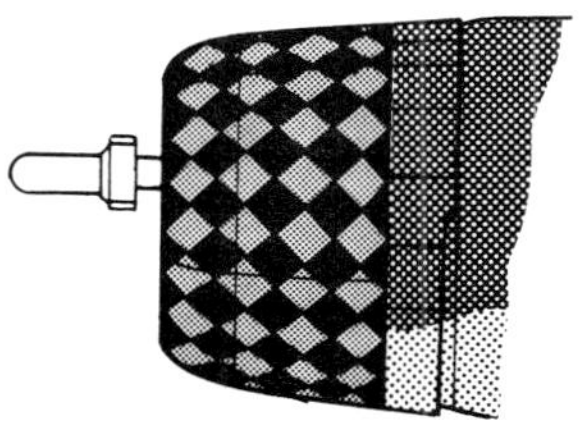

Standard yellow & black checkerboard (varying size squares) (from April 1944).

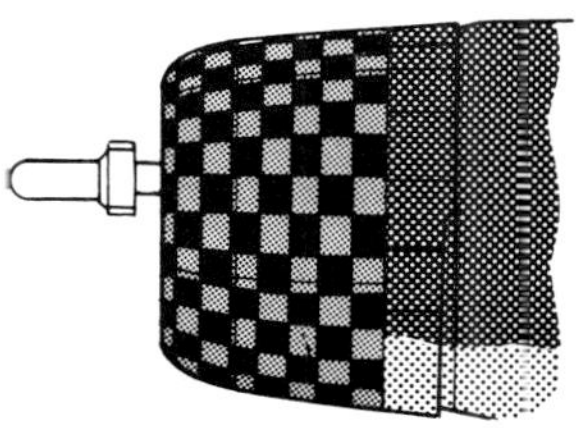

Non - standard checker-board on some P-47s.

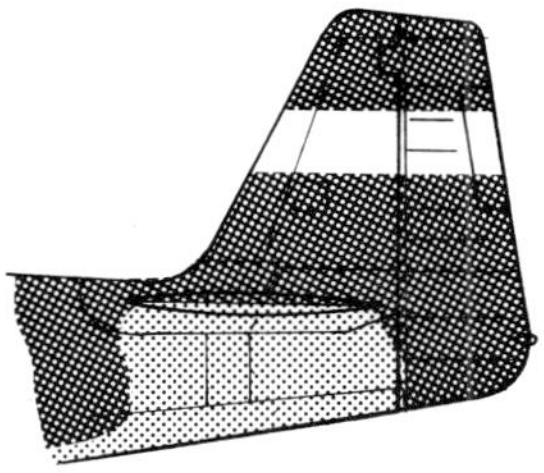

Standard P-51

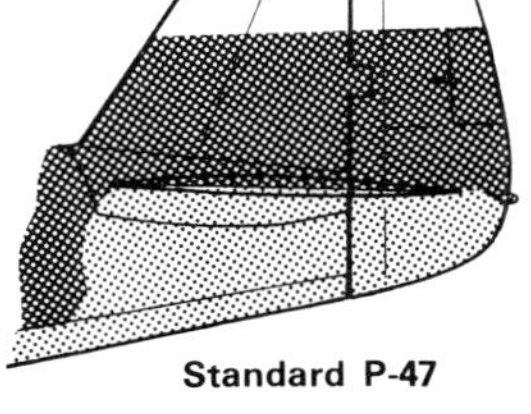

Standard P-47

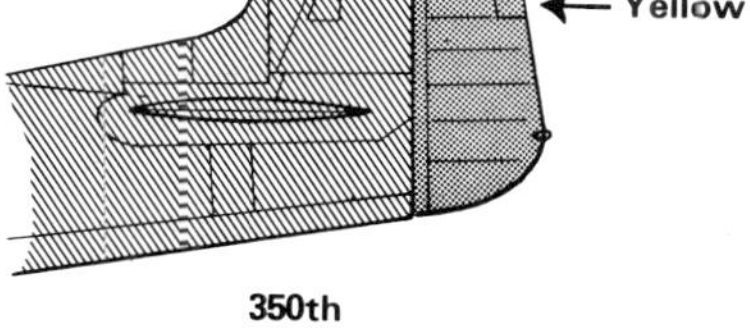

350th

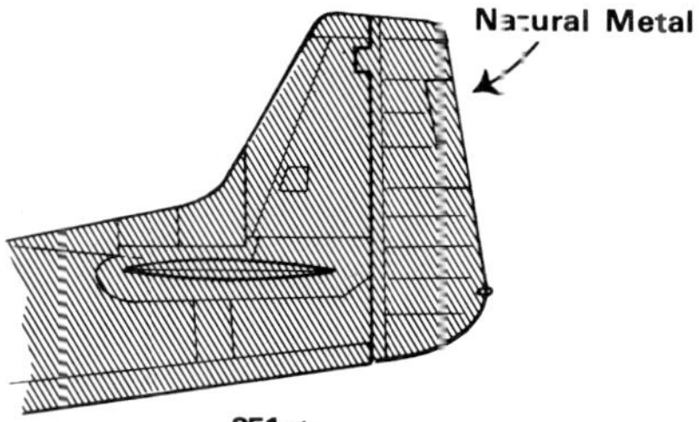

351st

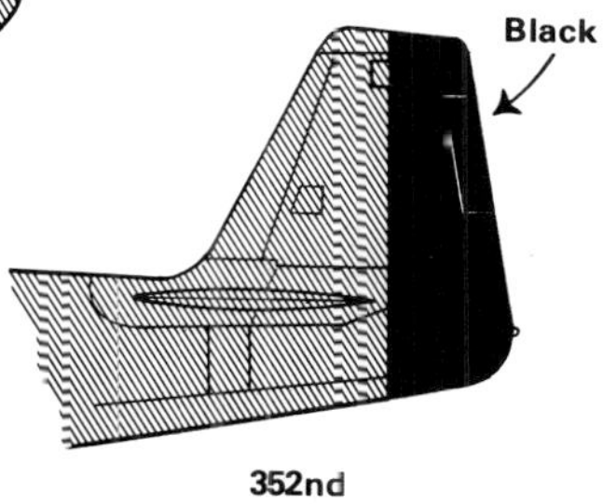

352nd

SQUADRON TAIL COLORS (from November 1944)

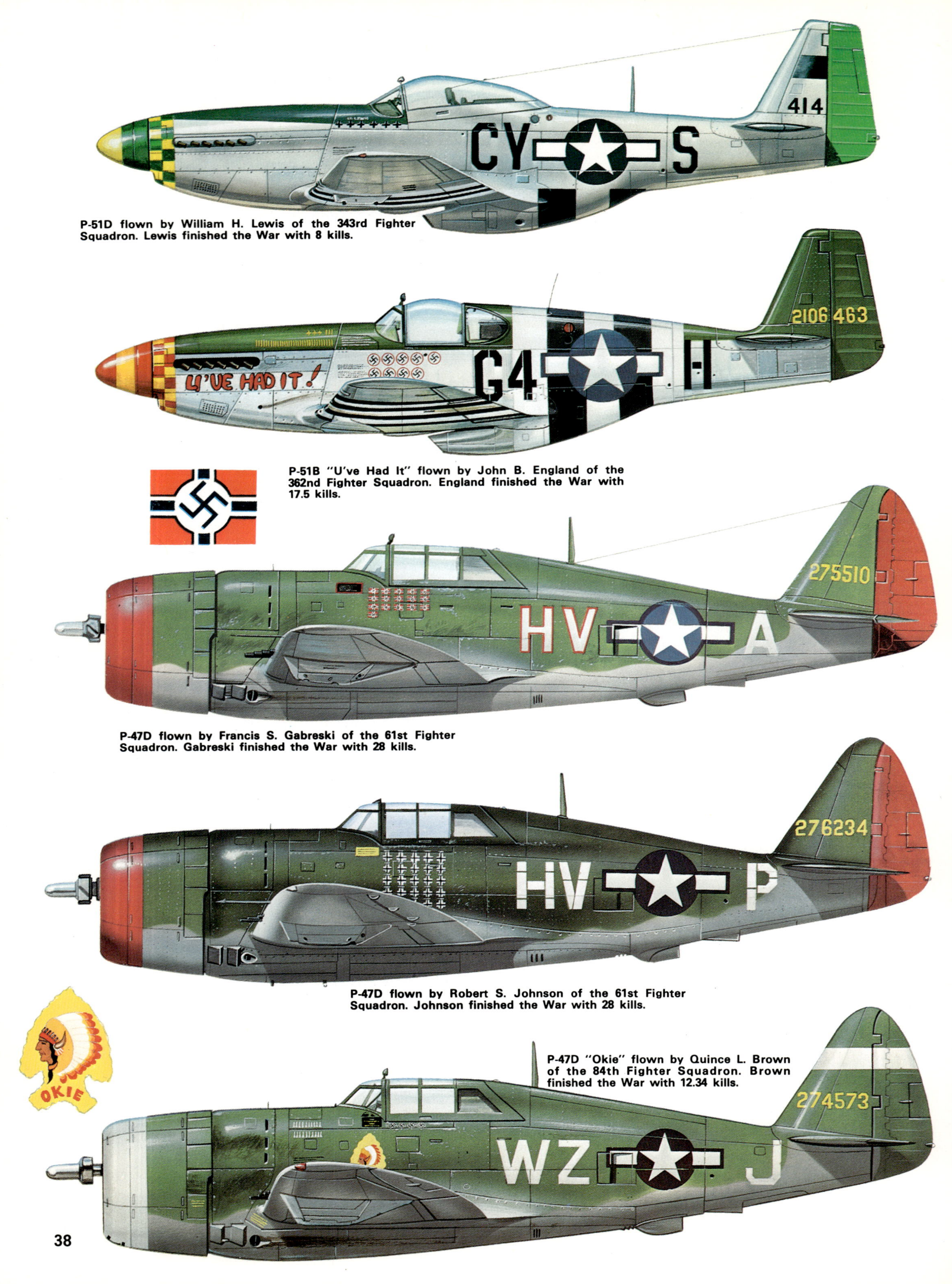

P-51D flown by William H. Lewis of the 343rd Fighter Squadron. Lewis finished the War with 8 kills.

P-51B "U've Had It" flown by John B. England of the 362nd Fighter Squadron. England finished the War with 17.5 kills.

P-47D flown by Francis S. Gabreski of the 61st Fighter Squadron. Gabreski finished the War with 28 kills.

P-47D flown by Robert S. Johnson of the 61st Fighter Squadron. Johnson finished the War with 28 kills.

P-47D "Okie" flown by Quince L. Brown of the 84th Fighter Squadron. Brown finished the War with 12.34 kills.

355th Fighter Group

The **355TH Fighter Group** was activated at Orlando, Florida on 12 November 1942 and trained there until February 1943. From there it moved first to Richmond, Virginia and then to Philadelphia, Pennsylvania before receiving orders to ship out for England. While still in the States the unit began to work up on the P-47 and it was with this fighter that the 355TH settled into its home in England — Steeple Morden - on 8 July 1943. This base was to be the Group's home throughout the entire war. The first combat mission was flown on 14 September. The Group continued to fly the P-47 in combat until March 1944. At that time the P-51s began to arrive and replace the older fighter type. The Mustang remained the mount of the Group until the end of hostilities. Though the 355TH scored well in the air, it was in the ground attack role that it really excelled. In this area, the 355TH led all Eighth Air Force outfits in the number of aircraft destroyed on the ground. The Group won a Distinguished Unit Citation for one attack on German airfields when it destroyed a large number of planes in the midst of snow squalls. During the period between its first mission and its last (25 April 1945) the **355TH Fighter Group** destroyed some 365½ enemy planes in the air and another 502½ on the ground. Losses for the Group totaled 175 aircraft.

Squadron Codes ● 354th - **WR**, 357th - **OS**, 358th - **YF**

HENRY W. BROWN (17.2) - Though born in Dallas, Texas, Brown claimed Washington, D.C. as his home town. His highest scoring day was 27 September 1944 when he shot down four German planes. Brown also scored a triple on 11 September and added doubles on two other occasions. On 3 October 1944 his plane was hit by flak and he bellied in in occupied territory and was made a prisoner. In addition to the two planes shown here, Brown also flew a P-47 nicknamed "Baby". This ship was also coded WR☆Z (42-74703) (Credit: USAF Museum, W. Smetzer).

WILLIAM J. HOVDE (10.5) - **Hovde, a native of Crookston, Minnesota, and his series of "Ole's" became dependable leaders in the 358TH Fighter Squadron. He put a fitting capstone on his combat career when he destroyed five German planes and shared a sixth northeast of Berlin on 5 December 1944. His planes were all named "Ole" and were coded YF☆I (Credit: D. Morris, W. Hovde).**

EVERETT W. STEWART (7.83) - **A native of Abiline, Kansas, he first served in the Pacific with the 18TH Fighter Group. Stewart served with the 352ND before taking command of the 355TH and later also led the 4TH Fighter Group. Though not among the highest scorers, he was one of the outstanding fighter leaders to emerge from the war. His aircraft with the 4TH is shown on the back cover (Credit: E. Stewart).**

JAMES E. DUFFY (5.2) - **Duffy wasn't one of the higher scorers in the Group, but he became one of the top lead pilots in his Squadron. The Montclair, New Jersey native downed an FW-190 on one occasion when he only had one of his guns firing. His plane was "Dragon Wagon" and carried both his air and ground victories (44-63764) (Credit: J. Vleit).**

FREDERICK R. HAVILAND (9.) - The Chicago, Illinois native did most of his scoring in the Summer and Fall of 1944, getting singles and doubles when he had the opportunity to mix it up with the enemy. Haviland was also a proficient strafer and had six enemy aircraft to his credit on the ground. The aircraft shown, "The Iowa Beaut", was flown by Haviland on several occasions but it was not his assigned aircraft (Credit: D. Morris).

CLAIBORNE H. KINNARD, JR. (8.) - Kinnard served with the 355TH through the end of October 1944 and then was assigned to command the 4TH Fighter Group. He remained in this job until December 1944. In February 1945 he returned to his original outfit as its commander. His aircraft with the 4TH was also named "Man O'War" and was coded QP☆A (44-14292).

ACES

NAME	SCORE	OTHER GROUPS
Henry W. Brown	17.2	
William J. Hovde	10.5	
Frederick R. Haviland, Jr.	9.	
John L. Elder	8.	
Claiborne H. Kinnard, Jr.	8.	4
Everett W. Stewart	7.83	352/4
Gordon M. Graham	7.	
Bert W. Marshall	7.	
Robert E. Woody	7.	
Henry S. Bille	6.	
William J. Cullerton	6.	
Norman E. Olson	6.	
Norman J. Fortier	5.83	
Walter J. Karoleski, Jr.	5.54	
Leslie D. Minchew	5.5	359
Raymond B. Myers	5.5	
James E. Duffy	5.2	
Charles W. Lenfest	5.	
James N. McElroy	5.	
Royce W. Priest	5.	
William F. Wilson	5.	

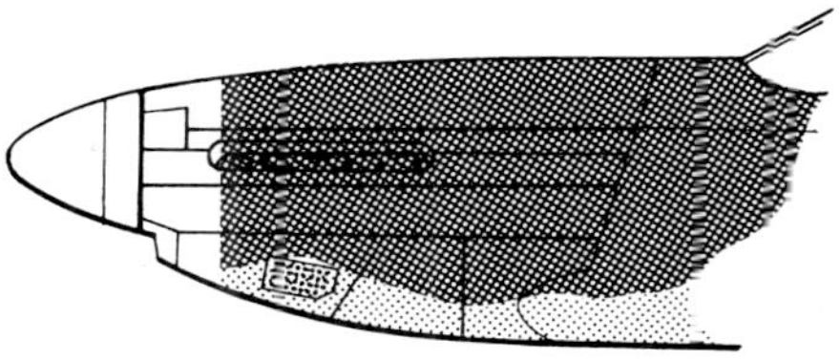

White spinner & 12 inch cowl band on P-51.

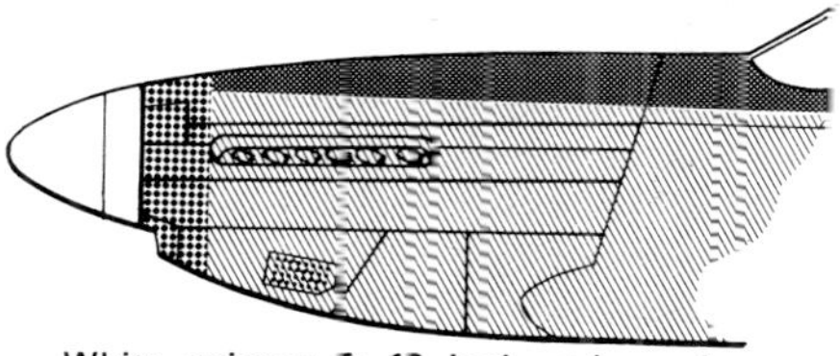

White spinner & 12 inch red cowl band for 354th squadron (from Nov. 44).

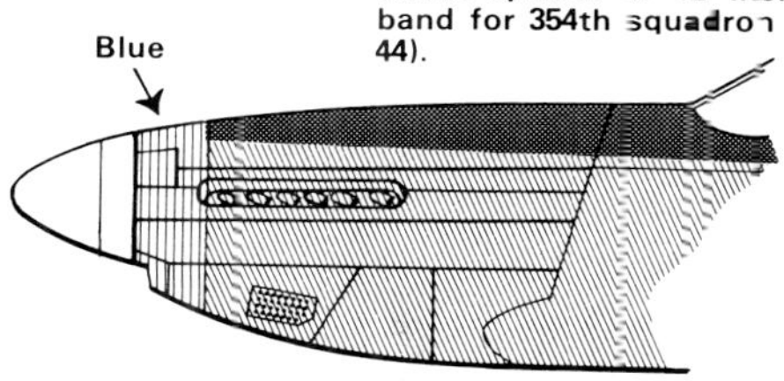

White spinner & 12 inch blue cowl band for 357th squadron (from Nov. 44).

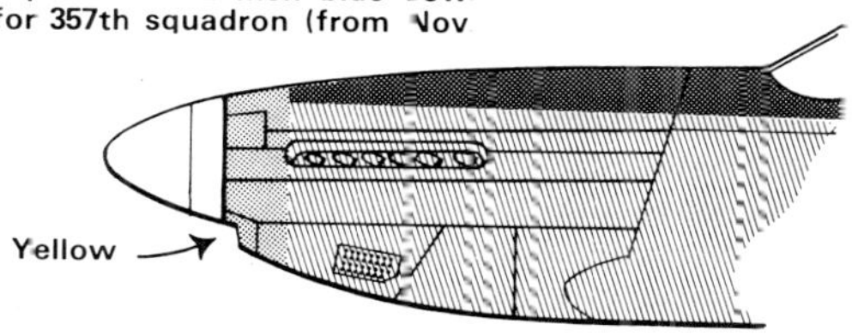

White spinner & 12 inch yellow cowl band for 358th squadron (from Nov. 44).

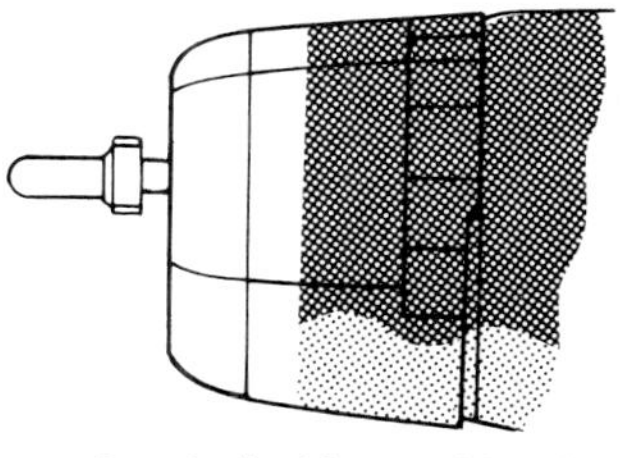

Standard white cowl band on P-47

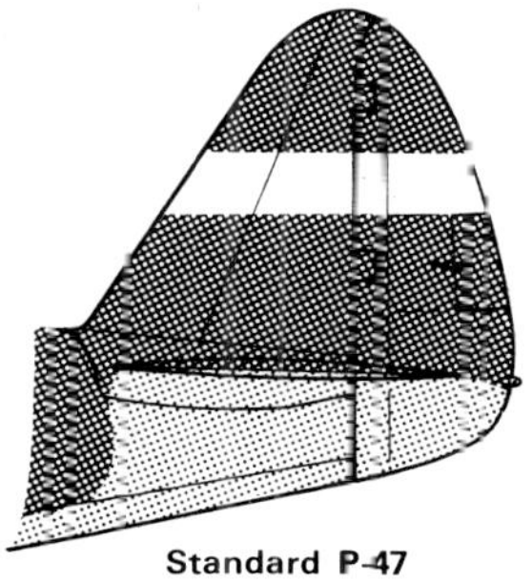

Standard P-47

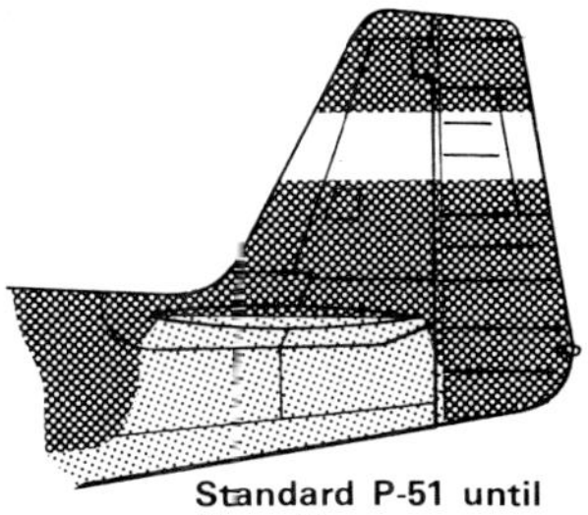

Standard P-51 until Nov. 44

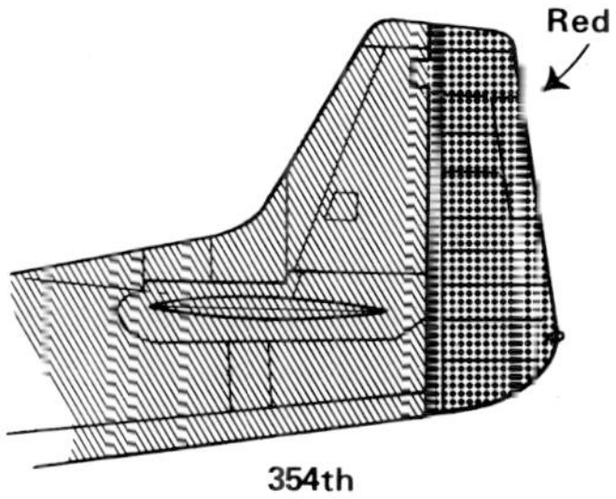

354th

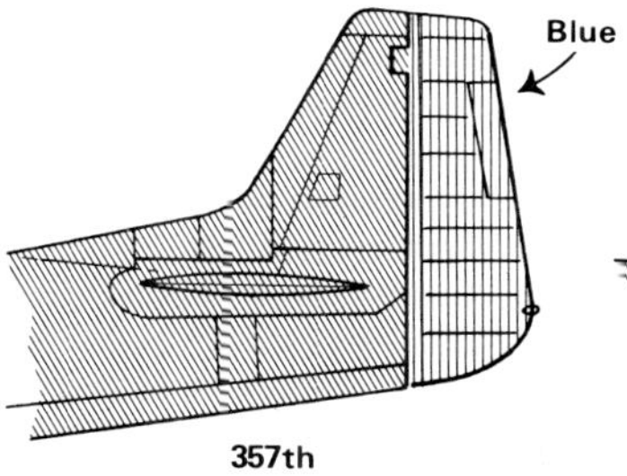

357th

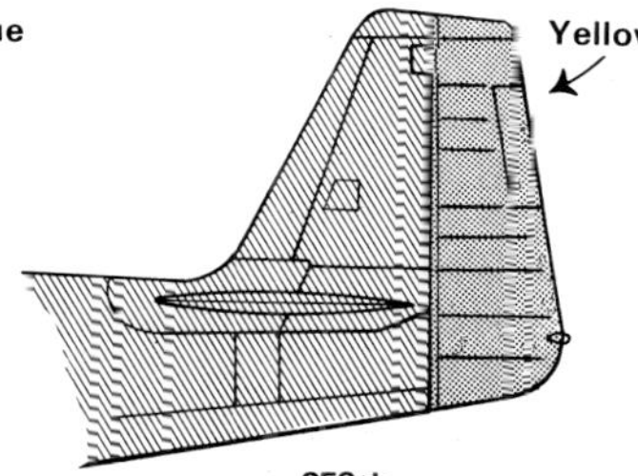

358th

SQUADRON TAIL COLORS (from November 1944)

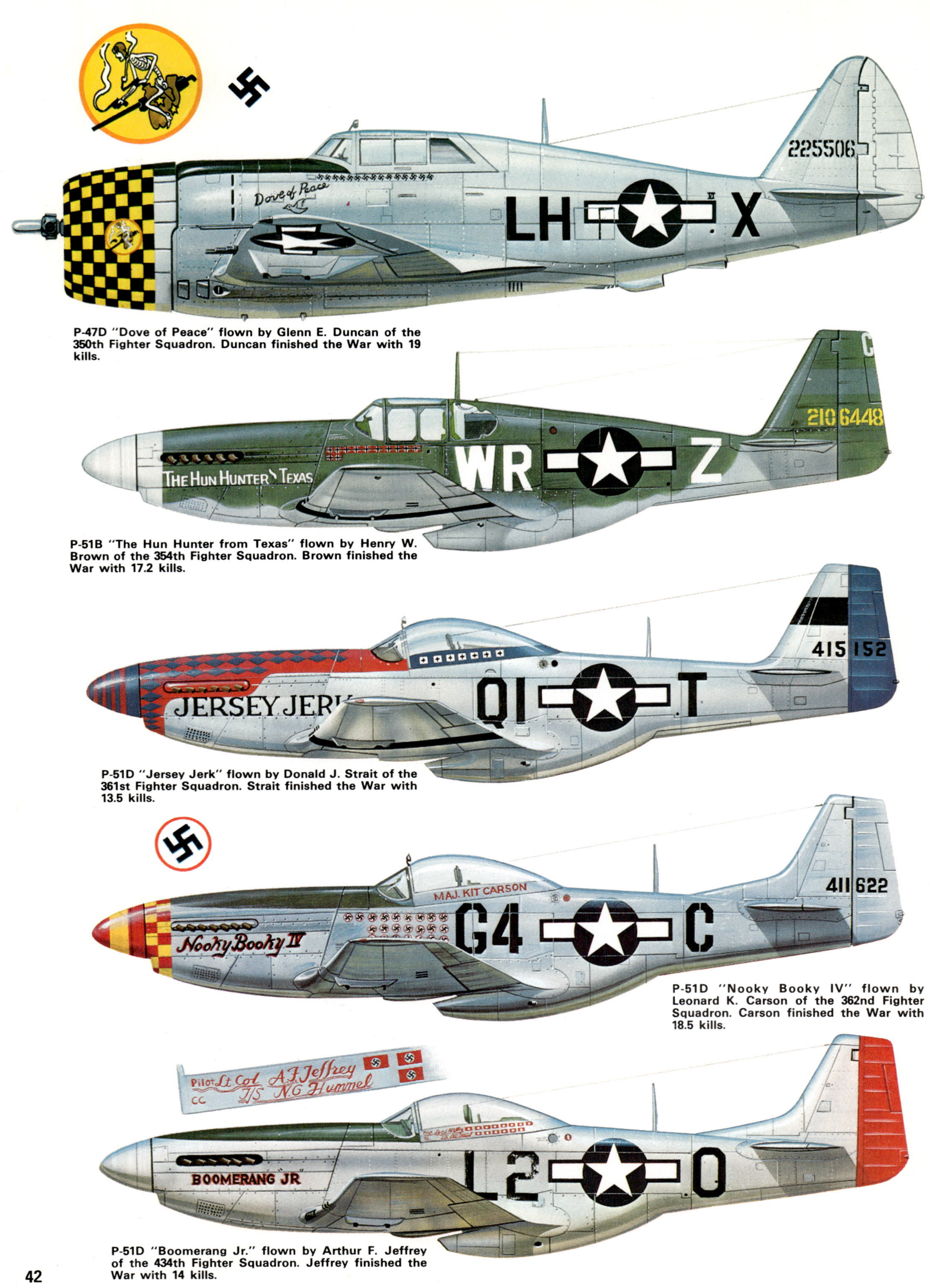

P-47D "Dove of Peace" flown by Glenn E. Duncan of the 350th Fighter Squadron. Duncan finished the War with 19 kills.

P-51B "The Hun Hunter from Texas" flown by Henry W. Brown of the 354th Fighter Squadron. Brown finished the War with 17.2 kills.

P-51D "Jersey Jerk" flown by Donald J. Strait of the 361st Fighter Squadron. Strait finished the War with 13.5 kills.

P-51D "Nooky Booky IV" flown by Leonard K. Carson of the 362nd Fighter Squadron. Carson finished the War with 18.5 kills.

P-51D "Boomerang Jr." flown by Arthur F. Jeffrey of the 434th Fighter Squadron. Jeffrey finished the War with 14 kills.

356th Fighter Group

The **356TH Fighter Group** was activated on 12 December 1942 at Westover Field, Massachusetts. Training continued there until March 1943 when the Group moved to Groton Field, Connecticut and began to train with P-47s. The outfit also served at two other State-side bases before shipping out for England in August 1943. As with several other Groups, the first home in England was Goxhill but the 356TH was only there for just over one month. The permanent home for the Group was Martlesham Heath and it settled in on 5 October 1943. The first of the Group's 413 combat missions was flown on 15 October 1943. The Distinguished Unit Citation was awarded to the Group for its actions in support of the airborne invasion of Holland on 17, 18 and 23 September 1944. The Group remained with the Thunderbolt until late November 1944 at which time the Group transitioned to the Mustang. The unit was not one of the higher scoring units in the Eighth Air Force either in the air or on the ground. A total of 201 German planes were destroyed in the air by the 356TH and another 75½ were destroyed on the ground. This total, 276½ enemy planes, was the lowest of any of the fifteen groups with the Eighth. Combat losses for the unit were 122 aircraft, the highest ratio of losses to victories in the Eighth.

Squadron Codes • 359th - **OC**, 360th - **PI**, 361st - **QI**

DONALD J. STRAIT (13.5) - The leading ace of the 356TH called Verona, New Jersey home. Strait rose to the rank of Major and command of the 361ST Fighter Squadron. Among his victories were doubles on 7 December 1944 and 14 February 1945. He was credited with 1½ victories on 28 November 1944. Strait's P-47, like his P-51, was coded QI☆T and named "Jersey Jerk". The serial number for his Thunderbolt was 42-76844 while that for his Mustang was 44-15152. (Credit: D. Strait, USAF).

ACES

NAME	SCORE	OTHER GROUPS
Donald J. Strait	13.5	
Wilbur R. Scheible	6.	
David F. Thwaites	6.	
Clinton D. Burdick	5.5	
Donald A. Baccus	5.	359
John W. Vogt Jr. *	8.	56

* Victories primarily with other units.

DONALD J. STRAIT

WILBUR R. SCHEIBLE (6.) - The Akron, Ohio native destroyed his first German aircraft on his fourth combat mission. He began his tour in June 1944 and he rose to the position of Group Operations Officer. His Mustang was coded QI☆Z and bore the serial number 42-76457 (Credit: W. Scheible).

DAVID F. THWAITES (6.) - Thwaites' hometown was Conshohocken, Pennsylvania. He joined the 356TH in December 1943 and by the time his tour was up in September 1944 he was a flight leader with some 115 combat missions under his belt. Thwaites had four Me-109s and an FW-190 to his credit. "Polly", his personal mount was coded QI☆L (42-75214). The name appeared on both sides of the cowling (Credit: D. Thwaites).

44

CLINTON D. BURDICK (5.5) - **This Mustang pilot from Brooklyn, New York had his biggest day on 14 January 1945. On this date he tangled with a gaggle of FW-190s and succeeded in destroying two of them and damaging two others. His second victory of the day was made while Burdick had but one gun firing.**

DONALD A. BACCUS (5.) - **Baccus began his tour of duty with the Eighth Air Force 356TH as a member of the 359TH Squadron. He eventually rose to command the 356TH in November 1944 and in April 1945 took command of the 359TH Fighter Group. All five of his victories were scored while Baccus was with his original outfit. The photo shows his plane while he was with the 359TH. He had a P-47 named "The Bloody Shaft" (OC ☆ T) and a P-51 (OC ☆ G) while with the 356TH. The latter was devoid of markings other than his victories. (Credit: D. Baccus).**

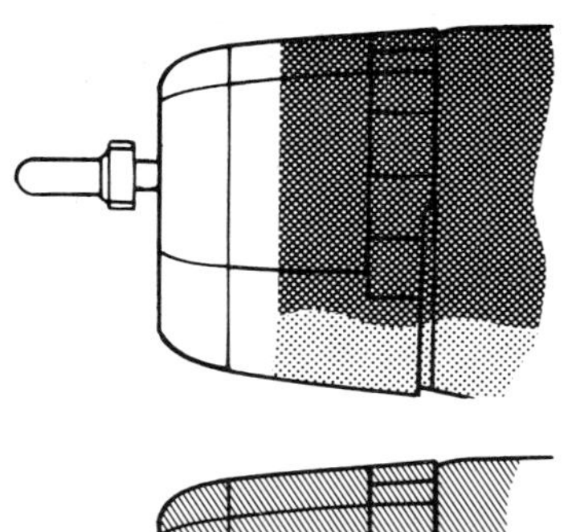

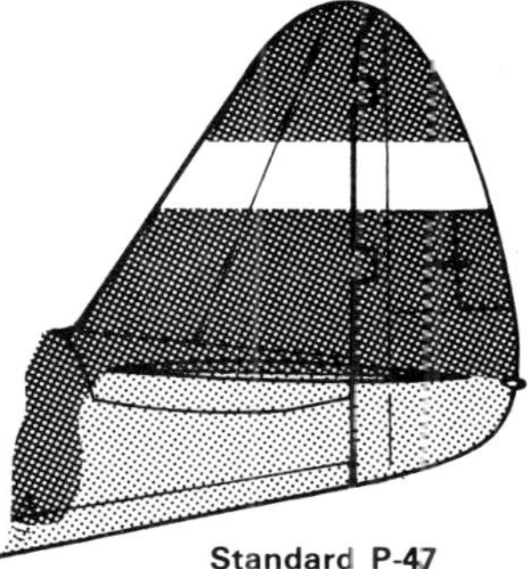

Cowl bands removed (or painted over on camouflaged P-47s) from April 1944.

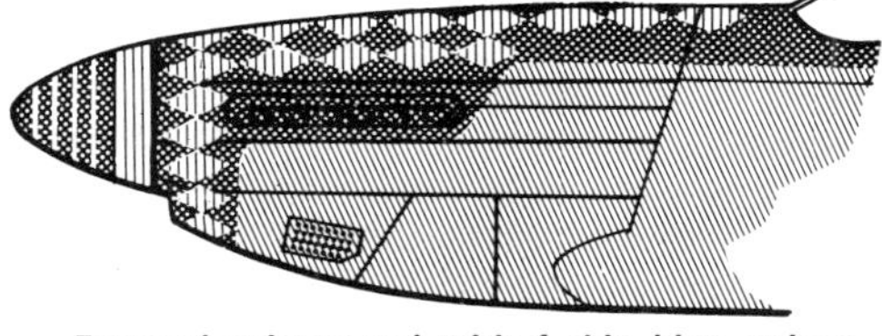

Forward spinner red with 4 thin blue stripes. Last 9 inches of spinner blue. 12 inch red cowl band with extension to windscreen super - imposed with medium blue diamonds. (from November 1944).

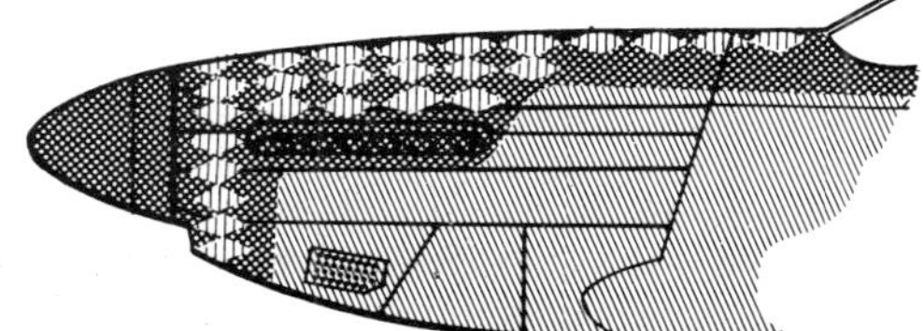

Spinner painted in squadron color (from February 1944).

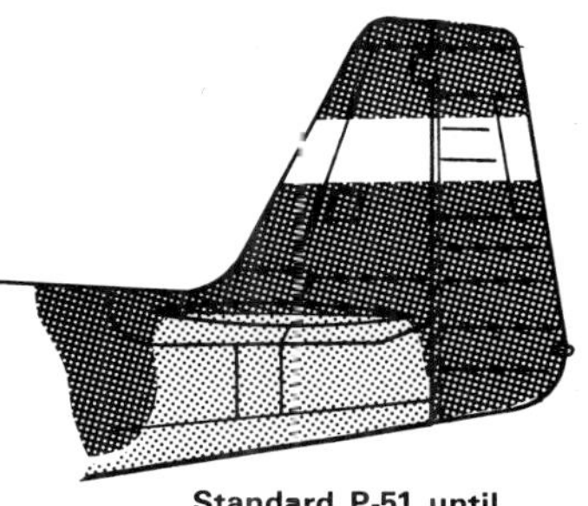

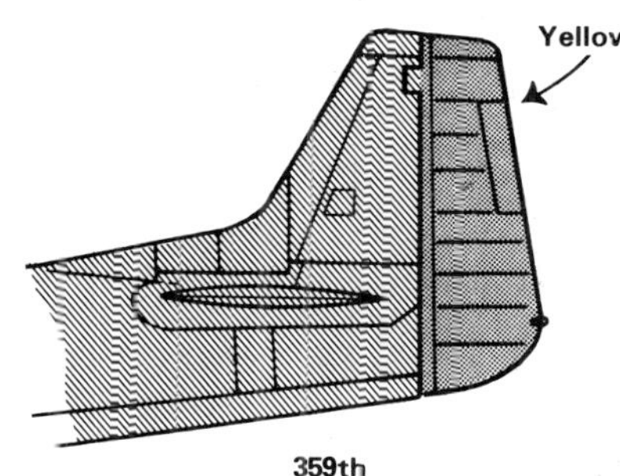

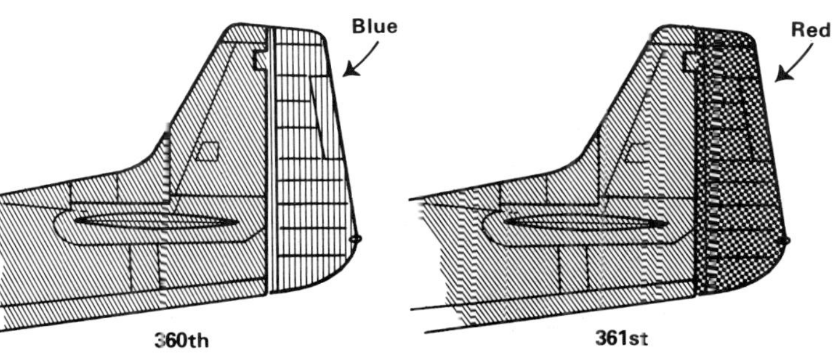

SQUADRON TAIL COLORS (from December 1944)

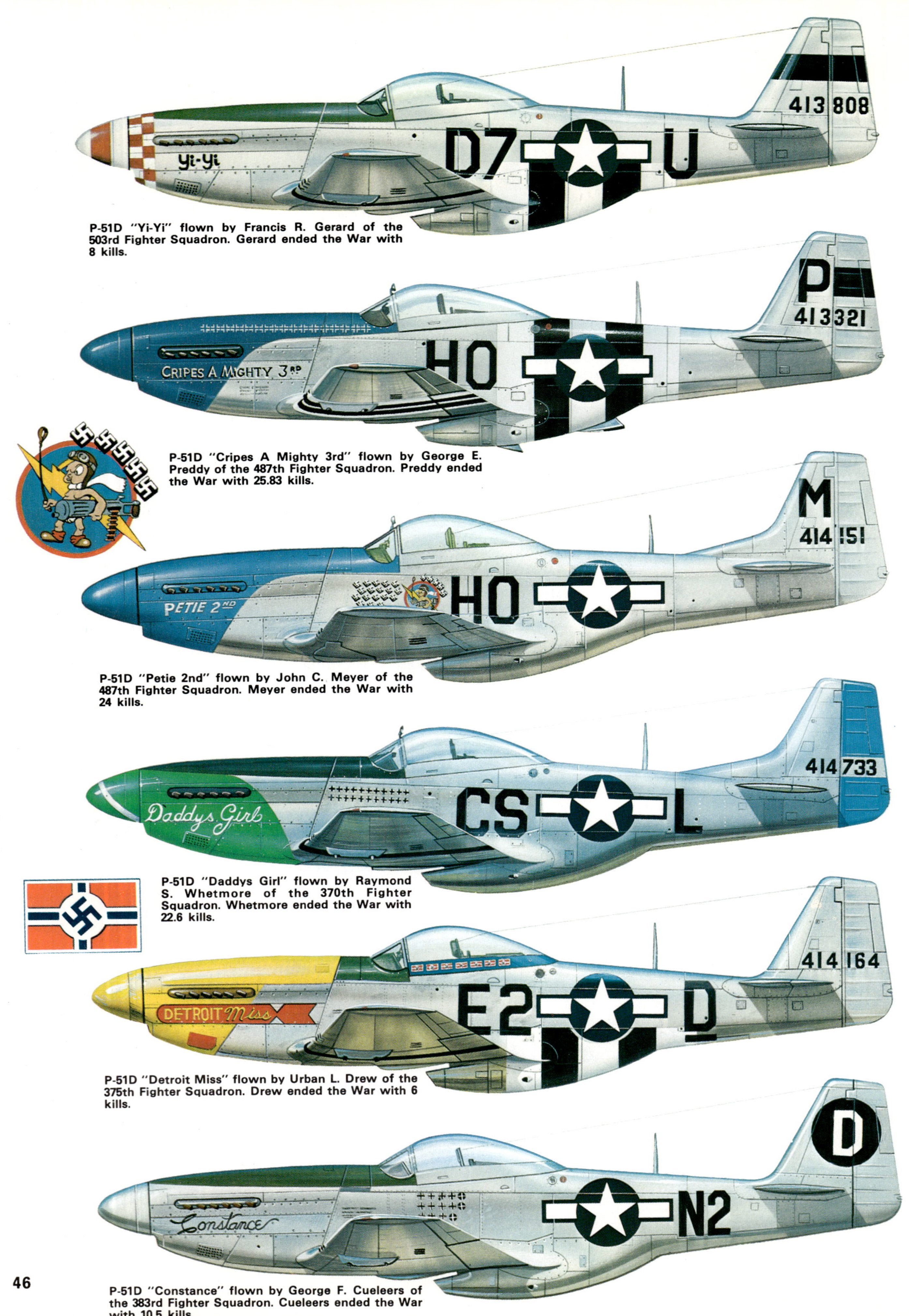

P-51D "Yi-Yi" flown by Francis R. Gerard of the 503rd Fighter Squadron. Gerard ended the War with 8 kills.

P-51D "Cripes A Mighty 3rd" flown by George E. Preddy of the 487th Fighter Squadron. Preddy ended the War with 25.83 kills.

P-51D "Petie 2nd" flown by John C. Meyer of the 487th Fighter Squadron. Meyer ended the War with 24 kills.

P-51D "Daddys Girl" flown by Raymond S. Whetmore of the 370th Fighter Squadron. Whetmore ended the War with 22.6 kills.

P-51D "Detroit Miss" flown by Urban L. Drew of the 375th Fighter Squadron. Drew ended the War with 6 kills.

P-51D "Constance" flown by George F. Cueleers of the 383rd Fighter Squadron. Cueleers ended the War with 10.5 kills.

357th Fighter Group

The **357TH Fighter Group** was activated on 1 December 1942 at Hamilton Field, California. The Group trained in P-39s and served at several other western bases in the United States before it shipped out for England in November 1943. The 356TH was initially assigned to the Ninth Air Force and based at Raydon from 30 November 1943. The Group began to re-equip with P-51Bs and since the Eighth Air Force saw the need to have this fighter, a swap was arranged with the Ninth. The 357TH was transferred to the Eighth in exchange for the 358TH Fighter Group. This exchange also brought about a change in station with the 357TH moving to Leiston. The Group was the first Eighth Air Force group to fly the P-51 in combat. Its first combat mission came on 11 February 1944 and it soon established itself as a top-scoring outfit. Only the 56TH Fighter Group scored more victories in the air and for the last year of the war the 357TH had the highest rate of aerial victories in the Eighth Air Force. The unit received a Distinguished Unit Citation for its outstanding escort of the bombers on 6 March and 29 June 1944. It also received a DUC for its actions on 14 January 1945. The 356TH flew the Mustang throughout its combat tour, ending the war in the K-model. In some 313 combat missions, the Group destroyed 609½ German planes in the air and 106½ on the ground for a loss of 128 aircraft.

Squadron Codes ● 362nd - **G4**, 363rd - **B6**, 364th - **C5**

LEONARD K. CARSON (18.5) - **A native of Clearlake, Iowa, Carson completed his tour as the top ace in the 357TH. Most of his victories were achieved during the last six months of the war. On 27 November 1944, he had his highest scoring day by downing five German planes (Credit: W. Smelzer).**

JOHN B. ENGLAND (17.5) - **England, from Caruthersville, Missouri, had several high scoring days including 27 November 1944 when he got four. He also had a triple and a 2½ victory mission to his credit. England rose to command the 362ND Squadron. His "U've Had It" was coded G4 ☆ H (42-106463) as was his later "Missouri Armada" (Credit: M. Olmstead).**

ROBERT W. FOY (17.) - Foy came from Oswego, New York. He scored doubles on 29 June 1944 and 14 January 1945. Foy also was credited with an Me-262 on 19 March 1945. Within a single two month period, he was twice pulled from the Channel by Air-Sea Rescue. His first mount, B6☆V had the serial number 44-13712 and pictured a girl in a bathing suit just above the name (Reluctant Rebel"). His "Little Shrimp" was also coded B6☆V (Credit: W. Smelzer, M. Olmstead).

CLARENCE E. ANDERSON (16.5) - This native of Newcastle, California flew two tours with the 357TH. He compiled a total of 116 missions between the two. Anderson scored three victories two separate times. All of his aircraft were coded B6☆S and at least the last two were named "Old Crow" (Credit: D. Weatherill).

ACES

NAME	SCORE	OTHER GROUPS	NAME	SCORE	OTHER GROUPS
Leonard K. Carson	18.5		Gerald E. Tyler	7.	
John B. England	17.5		Andrew J. Evans, Jr.	6.	
Robert W. Foy	17.		James J. Pascoe	6.	
Clarence E. Anderson	16.5		John F. Pugh	6.	
Richard A. Peterson	15.5		Orval J. Roberson	6.	
Donald H. Bochkay	14.84		Robert G. Schimanski	6.	
John A. Kirla	11.5		Frank L. Gailer	5.5	
Charles E. Yeager	11.5		Paul R. Hatala	5.5	
John A. Storch	10.5		William R. O'Brien	5.5	
Joseph E. Broadhead	10.		Leroy A. Ruder	5.5	
Fletcher E. Adams	9.5		Robert P. Winks	5.5	
Thomas L. Hayes	8.5	17PS	Raymond W. Bank	5.	
Otto D. Jenkins	8.5		John B. Carder	5.	
Alva C. Murphy	8.		Thomas L. Harris	5.	
Robert M. Shaw	8.		Charles D. Hauver	5.	
John L. Sublett	8.		Edwin W. Hiro	5.	
Charles E. Weaver	8.		Chester K. Maxwell	5.	
Glendon V. Davis	7.5		William C. Reese	5.	
Dale E. Karger	7.5		Morris A. Stanley	5.	
Robert H. Becker	7.		Jack R. Warren	5.	
James W. Browning	7.		John D. Landers *	14.5	49/55/78
Irwin H. Dregne	7.		John B. Murphy *	6.75	359
Gilbert M. O'Brien	7.				
Joseph F. Pierce	7.				

* Victories primarily with other units.

DONALD H. BOCHKAY (14.84) - From North Hollywood, California, Bochkay flew 123 combat missions during two tours with the 357TH. He was one of the few pilots that could list two Me-262s among his credits. Bochkay rose to command the 363RD Squadron. The aircraft shown here was the last of three for him and its serial number was 44-72244. His previous planes were coded B6☆F and were named "Alice in Wonderland" (43-6933) and "Speedball Alice" (44-15422). The second of these also carried the flying ace of spades insignia (Credit: M. Olmstead).

RICHARD A. PETERSON (15.5) - The native of Alexandra, Minnesota rose to the rank of major with the 357TH. Peterson scored most of his victories during the last nine months of the war. The two known aircraft of his were named "Hurry Home Honey" and both were coded C5☆T. His first plane, shown above had the serial number 44-13586 (Credit: M. Olmstead).

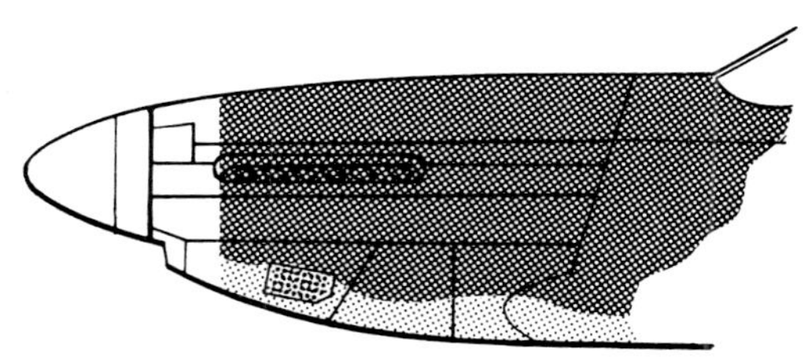

Standard white spinner & 12 inch cowl band.

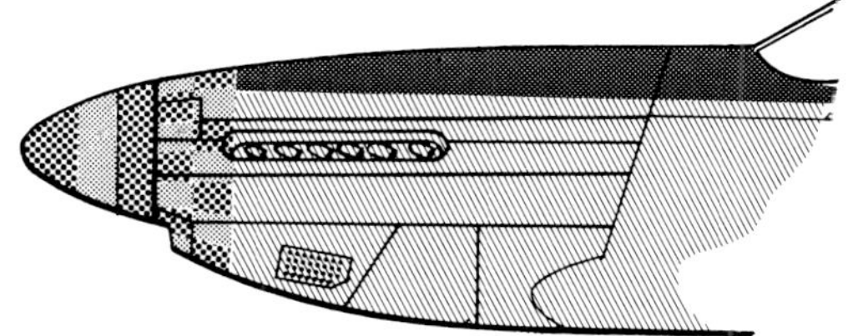

Red & yellow striped spinner. 12 inch red & yellow checkerboard cowl band.

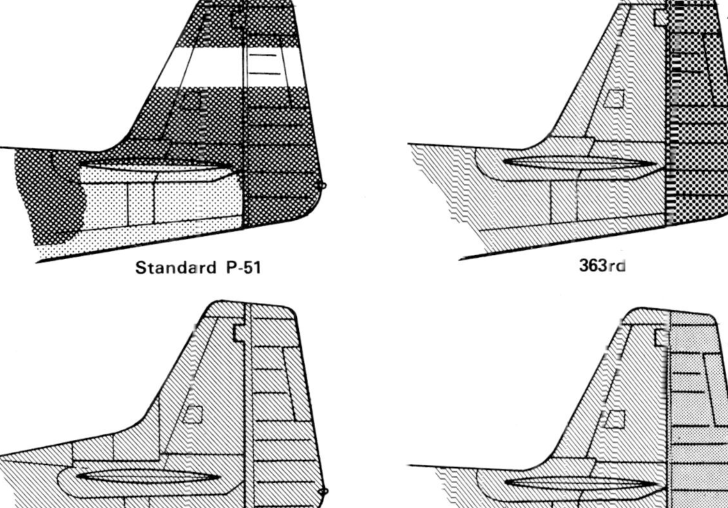

359th Fighter Group

The **359TH Fighter Group** was activated on 15 January 1943 at Westover Field, Massachusetts. The Group was assigned the Thunderbolt and it served at several bases in the northeastern part of the country before leaving for England in the early part of October 1943. The only home base for the 359TH overseas was East Waltham and the unit began flying combat missions from here on 13 December 1943. The 359TH entered combat in the P-47 but converted to the Mustang in early May 1944. All models of the Mustang were flown by the Group as they became available. The Group received the Distinguished Unit Citation for operations over Germany on 11 September 1944 when it protected a formation of bombers against a large number of German fighters. The 359TH Fighter Group flew some 346 combat missions over enemy territory during which it shot down 253 German planes. The Group also destroyed an additional 98 aircraft on the ground. The Group lost some 106 of its own planes during its combat tour.

Squadron Codes ● 368th - **CV**, 369th - **IV**, 370th - **CS**

ACES

NAME	SCORE	OTHER GROUPS
Raymond S. Wetmore	22.6	
George A. Doersch	10.5	
Robert J. Booth	8.	
Claude J. Crenshaw	7.	
Benjamin H. King	7.	347
John B. Murphy	6.75	357
Cyril W. Jones	6.	
Leslie D. Minchew	5.5	355
William F. Collins	5.	
Ralph L. Cox	5.	
Niven K. Cranfill	5.	
William R. Hodges	5.	
Robert M. York	5.	
Roy W. Evans *	6.	4
Donald A. Baccus *	5.	356

* Victories primarily with other units.

RAYMOND S. WETMORE (22.6) - Wetmore was a native of Kerman, California and ended the war as the top ace of the 359TH Fighter Group. He was one of the original pilots with the outfit and scored his last victory on 15 March 1945. This victory was over an Me-163 and was the last of four kills of this type scored by Eighth Air Force pilots during the war. His P-51, "Daddy's Girl" was coded CS☆L (44-14733). The P-47 shown was his first aircraft. As can be seen in the third shot, his victories were carried on the canopy at one time. This may have been on "Daddy's Girl" or it may have been a later plane (Credit: USAF).

CLAUDE J. CRENSHAW (7.) - Crenshaw of Monroe, Louisiana liked to get them in the air and on the ground. He had his greatest day in the air on 21 November 1944 when he ripped into a gaggle of German fighters and downed four of them. He finally had to break off when he ran out of ammunition. His aircraft, "Louisiana Heat Wave" was coded IV☆I (44-13606) (Credit: C. Crenshaw).

(Above & top right) GEORGE A. DOERSCH (10.5) - The native of Seymore, Wisconsin flew 410 combat missions. On his first mission in the P-51 he scored a double even though he had only two short hops in the new fighter. Doersch had a close call on one strafing mission when his prop struck the ground. He somehow regained control and made it home. "Ole Goat" was coded CV☆R. The plane shown with the bent prop was CS☆D (42-103345) (Credit: G. Doersch, D. Morris).

JOHN B. MURPHY (6.75) - **A native of Darlington, South Carolina, Murphy often led the 359TH into battle. As a combat leader his performance was excellent and as a combat pilot his score rose steadily whenever the opportunity presented itself. On 16 August 1944 he downed one of the vaunted Me-163s and damaged another (Credit: W. Smelzer).**

(Right & below) ROBERT J. BOOTH (8.) - Booth was a native of Waukesha, Wisconsin. He was rated as one of the best acrobatic pilots in the Eighth Air Force and downed all eight enemy aircraft he battled including a triple on one occasion. Booth finally was downed by ground fire on 8 June 1944 and spent the rest of the war as a POW.

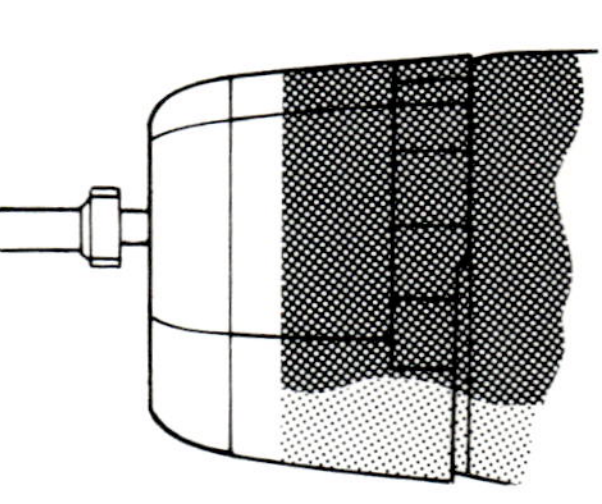
Standard white cowl band

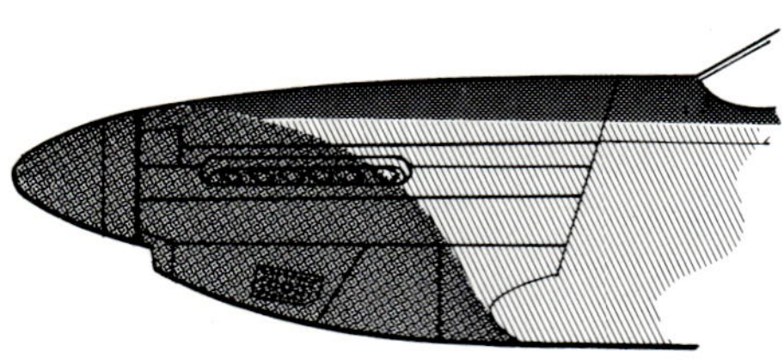
Green cowl swept down and back (from late 1944).

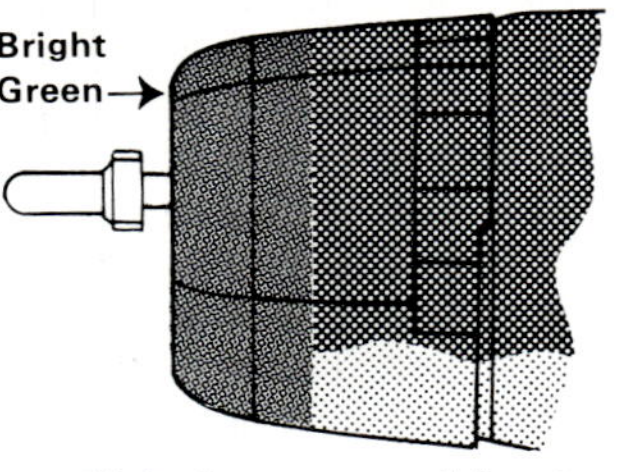

24 inch green cowl band (from March 1944).

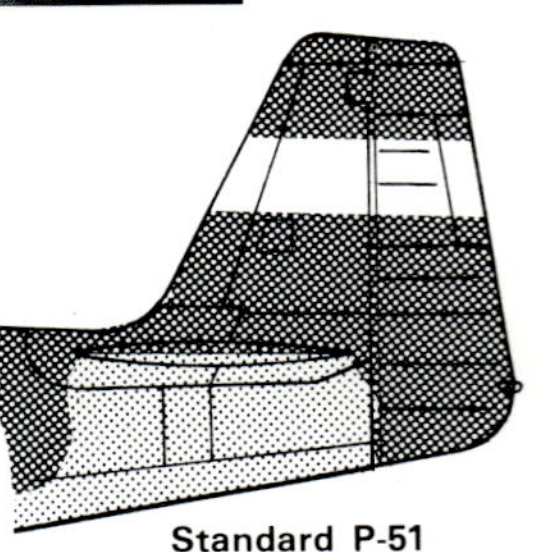
Standard P-51

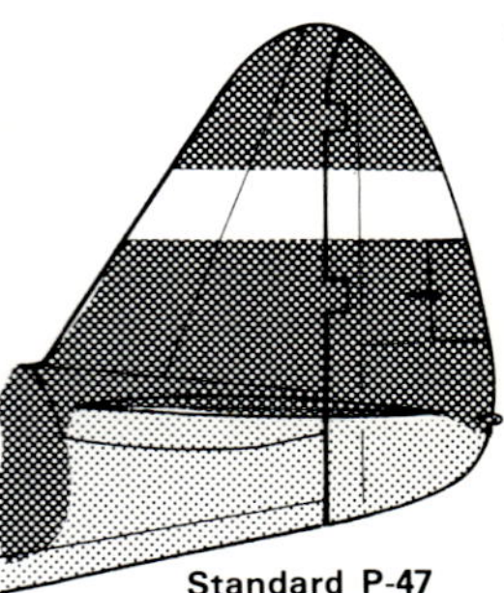
Standard P-47

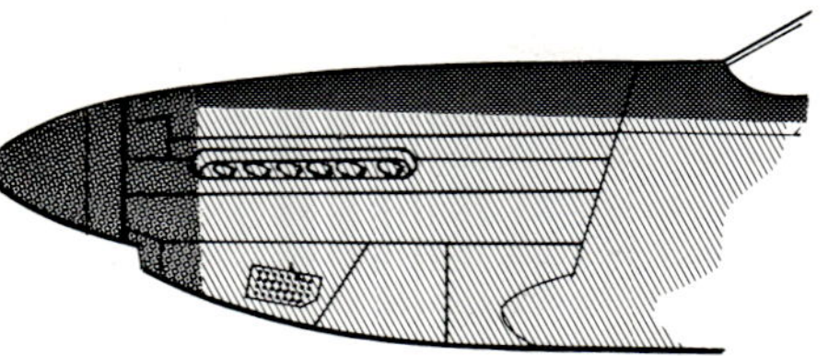
Green spinner & 12 inch green cowl band.

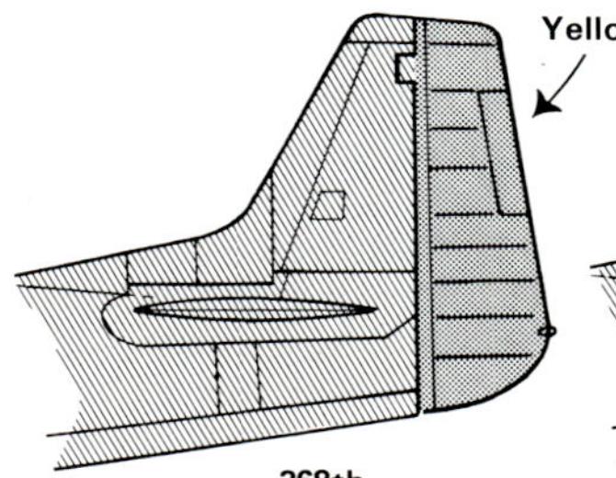

368th   369th

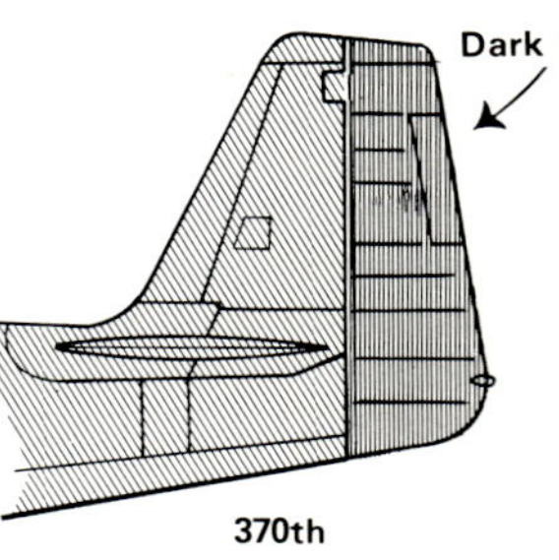

370th

SQUADRON TAIL COLORS (from November 1944)

361st Fighter Group

The **361ST Fighter Group** was activated on 10 February 1943 at Richmond AAB, Virginia. During the spring and summer of 1943 the Group moved to several bases in the eastern United States as it worked up on the P-47. The Group shipped out for overseas duty in November 1943 and settled into its first home in England, Bottisham, on 30 November. The Group remained at Bottisham for some ten months and then moved to Little Walden (26 September 1944). In early 1945 the unit was transferred to the Continent and operated from St. Dizier and later from Chievres. In early April the Group returned to England and again took up residence at Little Walden. The 361ST flew its first mission on 21 January 1944 and was the last Thunderbolt group to join the Eighth Air Force. The outfit operated this plane until May 1944 at which time it began conversion to the P-51. The Group flew a total of 441 combat missions during which its pilots were credited with the destruction of 226 German planes in the air and 105 more on the ground. The losses suffered by the 361ST were 81 aircraft.

Squadron Codes ● 374th - **B7**, 375th - **E2**, 376th - **E9**

ACES

NAME	SCORE	OTHER GROUPS
Dale F. Spencer	9.5	
William R. Beyer	9.	
Urban L. Drew	6.	414
Wallace E. Hopkins	6.	
William T. Kemp	6.	
Victor E. Bocquin	5.	
George L. Merritt	5.	
William J. Sykes	5.	
George R. Vanden Heuval	5.	
John D. Landers *	14.5	49/55/357/78
Joseph J. Kruzel *	5.5	17PS/49

* Victories primarily with other units.

DALE F. SPENCER (9.5) - Spencer, who called Corry, Pennsylvania home, liked to get his victories in clusters. His biggest day occured on 29 May 1944 when he encountered a bevy of Me-410s attacking the bombers. Spencer not only broke up the attack but sent four of them down in flames. His P-51 was coded E9☆D (43-24808). The Thunderbolt shown may have been his first aircraft (Credit: USAF).

WILLIAM R. BEYER (9.) - The Danville, Pennsylvania flyer had his biggest day on 27 September 1944 when he got into a gaggle of FW-190s and outmaneuvered them to claim five of their number. Beyer's aircraft was coded E9☆N and bore the serial number 44-14144.

WILLIAM T. KEMP (6.) - On 20 July 1944, Kemp had succeeded in destroying an Me-109 and had begun an attack on an FW-190 when three of his guns jammed. Ignoring this slight problem, Kemp closed in to a range of 15 yards and blasted the German plane from the sky. His aircraft was coded E2☆K (44-14278) and was named "Betty Lee II". Kemp is on the left of the first row (Credit: W. Smelzer).

WALLACE E. HOPKINS (6.) - Hopkins was born in Washington, Georgia and flew a total of 76 combat missions with the 361ST. The first of these came on 11 January 1944. He rose to the post of Deputy Group Commander. His P-51B was coded B7 ☆ H (42-106655) and his D-model, coded the same, had the serial number 44-13704. The latter plane is shown on the back cover (Credit: USAF).

URBAN L. DREW (6) - The Detroit, Michigan native was an instructor in P-51s before he joined the 361ST. He came to the Group just after D-Day and flew with it until November 1944. Drew had the unique distinction of destroying two Me-262s in the air on a single mission. He achieved this feat 8 October 1944 when he bounced the German jets just as they were taking off. After his tour in the ETO, Drew was transferred to the Pacific with the 414TH Fighter Group. His aircraft was coded E2☆D (44-14164) (Credit: U. Drew).

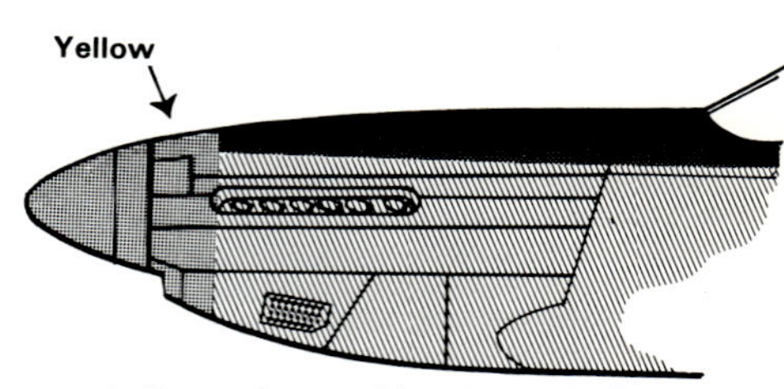

Yellow spinner with color extending back on the nose for 12 inches.

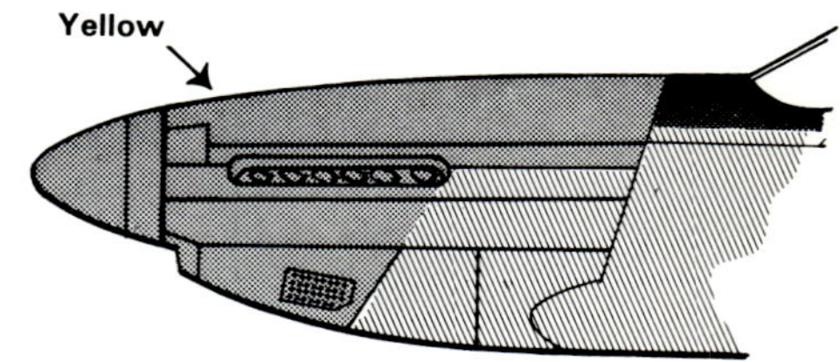

Yellow extended to windscreen from July/August 1944 on some aircraft.

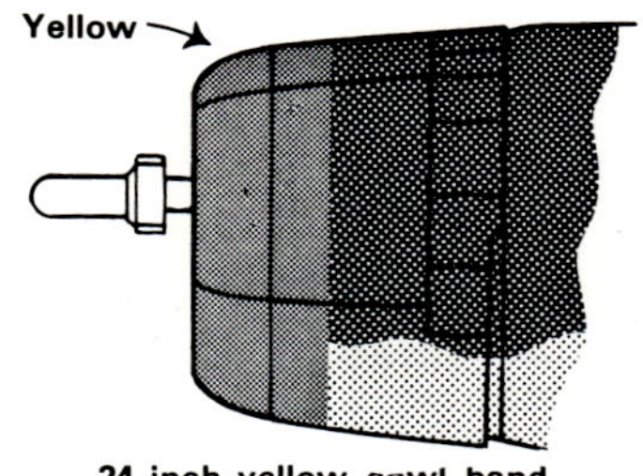

24 inch yellow cowl band from late March 1944. Prior to this the band was the standard white.

Standard P-47

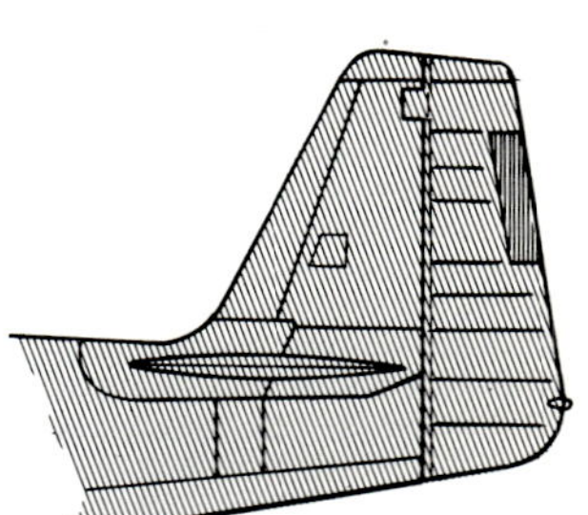

Trim tab in sq. color on some aircraft

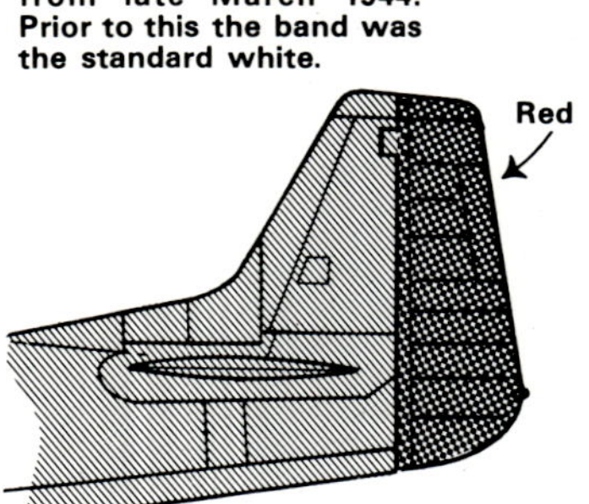

374th

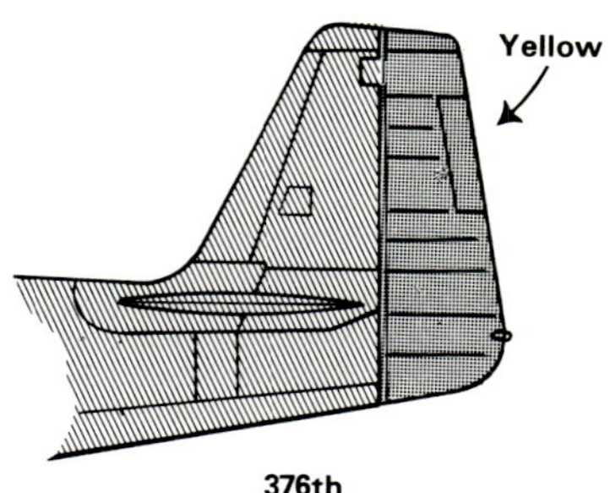

375th

376th

SQUADRON TAIL COLORS (November 1944 on)

364th Fighter Group

HISTORY

The **364TH Fighter Group** was activated on 1 June 1943 at Glendale, California The training period for the Group took place at various California bases as the unit worked up on the P-38. Orders finally arrived for the Group to prepare for overseas duty and in January 1944 it headed for Europe. The 364TH was assigned to Honington for the entire war period. The first combat mission came for the Group on 3 March 1944. It was awarded the Distinguished Unit Citation for an escort mission on 27 December 1944 when it dispersed a large force of German fighters that attacked the bomber formation the 364TH was guarding on a raid to Frankfort. Along with the normal escort duties the Group also flew air-sea rescue missions. The outfit continued to operate the Lightning until the latter part of July 1944. At this time the Group began to receive the Mustang and continued to fly the P-51 until the end of the war. The 364TH Fighter Group flew 342 missions. The number of aircraft destroyed was 449½ of which 255½ were brought down in aerial combat. Losses for the Group were 134 aircraft.

Squadron Codes ● 383rd - **N2**, 384th - **5Y**, 385th - **5E**

GEORGE F CUELEERS (10.5) - The top ace of the 364TH came from Bridgeton, New Jersey. Cueleers flew a total of 103 missions during his combat tour. His highest scoring day came when he downed four Me-109s in combat. On another occasion, he was credited with an Me-262. His P-38 may have carried the same codes as his P-51 (N2☆D). The serial number on Lightning is only partially known (42-680?) and no serial number showed on his Mustang (Credit: USAF).

ERNEST E. BANKEY (9) - Ernie Bankey was a native of Toledo, Ohio. He had been a consistent scorer during his days with the 364TH and on 27 December 1944, he made a classic radio call: "I've got 50 Jerries cornered over Bonn." In the ensuing fight, one that took him down to the steeple tops of the city, he shot down five of the enemy planes and shared a sixth with another pilot. His "Lucky Lady VII" was coded N2☆B and it carried the serial number 44-73045 (Credit: USAF, E. Bankey).

JAMES M. FOWLE (8.) - **One of Fowle's eight victories came on 2 November 1944. An Me-109 came at him from dead ahead but decided not to press the attack. As the German fighter banked to the right, Fowle was able to put a three second burst in the enemy's belly and knocked him from the sky. His "Terry Claire II" was coded 5Y☆Q and may have carried the serial number 44-14184 (Credit: USAF, D. Robinson).**

SAMUEL J. WICKER (7) - Wicker had three victories to his credit when he led the 364TH into battle on his last mission. The Luftwaffe was up in force and the Muskogee, Oklahoma native took his Mustangs into the middle of the fray. Wicker shot down two, terrorized a third into bailing out of his plane and just plain flew his fourth victim to the point where he lost control and crashed.

JOHN W. LOWELL (7.5) - Lowell flew two combat tours with the 364TH. His first mission came on 4 March 1943 and he was acting Group Commander for a one month period in the Fall of 1944. The serial number for "Penny", the plane he flew during his second tour, was 44-63263.

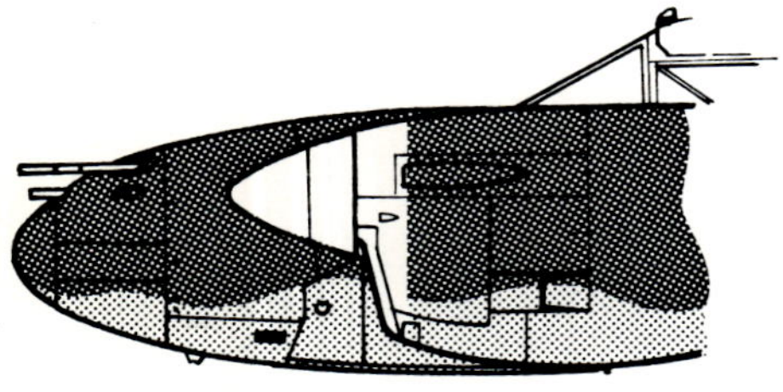

White spinners & 12 inch cowl bands.

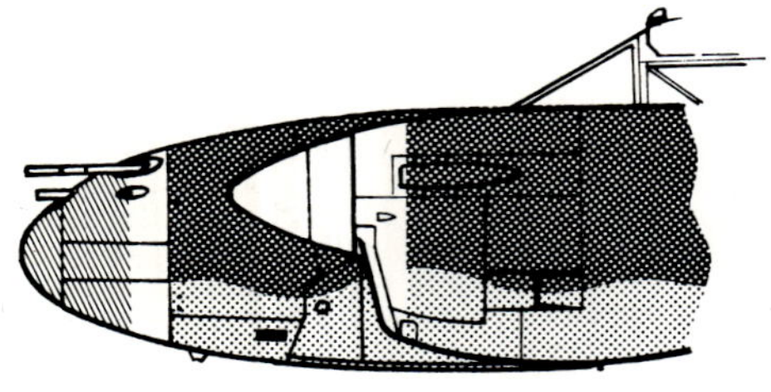

Droop-snoot decoy markings (from April 1944).

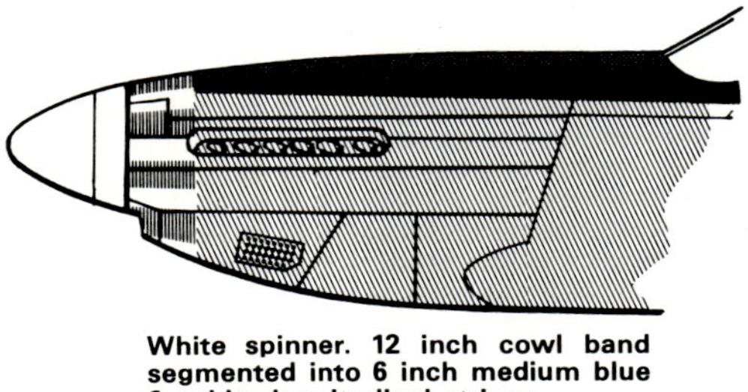

White spinner. 12 inch cowl band segmented into 6 inch medium blue & white longitudinal stripes.

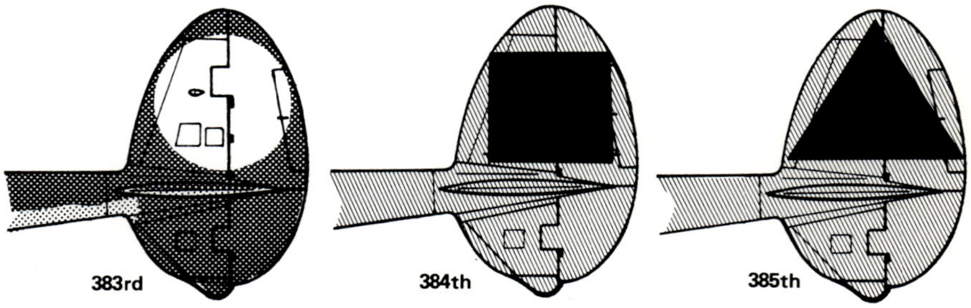

ACES

NAME	SCORE	OTHER GROUPS
George F. Cueleers	10.5	
Ernest E. Bankey, Jr.	9.5	
James M. Fowle	8.	
John W. Lowell	7.5	
Gilbert L. Jamison	7.	
Samuel J. Wicker	7.	
William F. Crombie	5.	
Eugene P. Roberts, Jr. *	9.	78

* Victories primarily with other units.

383rd   384th   385th

P-38 SQUADRON TAIL MARKINGS

383rd   384th   385th

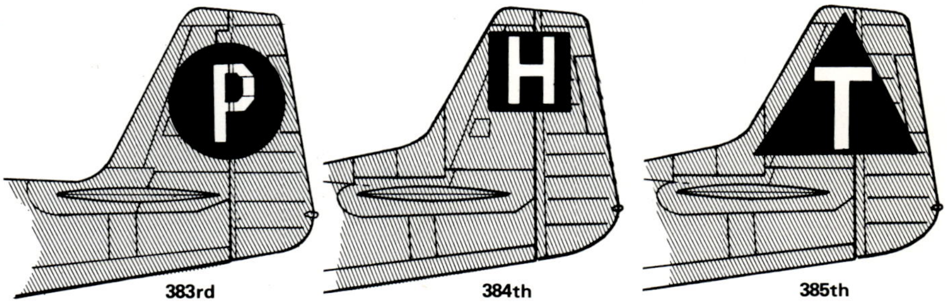

P-51 SQUADRON TAIL MARKINGS

479th Fighter Group

The last fighter group to join the Eighth Air Force was the **479TH**. The Group was activated on 15 October 1943 at Glendale, California and spent most of its training period at bases in California. It sailed for Europe in May 1944 and arrived at its only home in England, Wattisham, on 15 May 1944. The Eighth Air Force was preparing for the D-Day invasion, so the Group had a shorter period of pre-combat preparation than most groups. It flew its first combat mission on 26 May just eleven days after it had arrived. The unit had received P-38s while in the States and it was in this type that the Group went to war. The 479TH converted to the Mustang in September 1944 and continued to fly the P-51 until the end of the war. The Group received the Distinguished Unit Citation for the destruction of numerous aircraft on airfields in France on 18 August and 5 September and during an aerial battle near Munster on 26 September 1944. Captain Art Jeffrey of the outfit was the first pilot in the Eighth to battle the enemy jet aircraft and the Group also had the last German plane claimed by an Eighth Air Force pilot (Hilton Thompson). Though the unit had the least kills in the air (155) of any Eighth outfit, its 279 ground victories ranked the Group above average. The unit also lost the least number of planes (69).

Squadron Codes ● 434th - **L2**, 435th - **J2**, 436th - **B9**

ACES

NAME	SCORE	OTHER GROUPS
Arthur F. Jeffrey	14.	
Robin Olds	13.	
George W. Gleason	12.	
Richard G. Candelaria	6.	
Hubert A. Zemke *	17.75	56
Sydney S. Woods *	10.	49/4

* Victories primarily with other units.

ARTHUR F. JEFFREY (14.) - Jeffrey began his combat with the 479TH flying P-38s and by the end of the war was the leading ace in the Group. He was the first Eighth Air Force fighter pilot to do battle with the Me-163. On, this occasion, 29 July 1944, he came away with credit for a victory. Jeffrey scored a triple on 17 December 1944. His plane is shown in the color section (Credit: A. Jeffrey).

ROBIN OLDS (13) - Olds was the son of Major General Robert Olds and had spent his younger years moving from base to base. Nine of his victories were scored in P-38s, making him the top gun in this plane in the Eighth Air Force. His biggest day came on 25 August 1944 when he scored a triple. The aircraft shown here, "Scat VI" was coded L2☆W (44-72922) (Credit: J. Vleit).

GEORGE W. GLEASON (12) - George Gleason of Montrose, Colorado seemed to get his victories in clusters and really began to score once the 479TH got the P-51. His biggest day came on 26 September 1944 when he blasted three Me-109s from the sky and damaged another.

HUBERT A. ZEMKE (17.75) - Zemke was best known for his exploits with the 56TH Fighter Group but he did command the 479TH from 12 August to 30 October 1944. On the latter date he went down due to engine failure and was made a POW. Zemke flew the P-38 shown here and a P-51 while with the 479TH. Both were coded J2☆Z and the serial number on the Lightning was 43-28823 (Credit: R.A. Johnson).

SYDNEY S. WOODS (10.) - Woods was another of the pilots who flew in the Pacific (49TH Fighter Group) before coming to the Eighth Air Force. One of his victories came while he was with the 479th. His biggest day came while he was with the 4th Fighter Group when he shot down five enemy planes. The photo on the left shows his P-38 with the 479th (L2☆M) while that on the right shows his five victory aircraft (44-72251) (Credit: S. Woods).

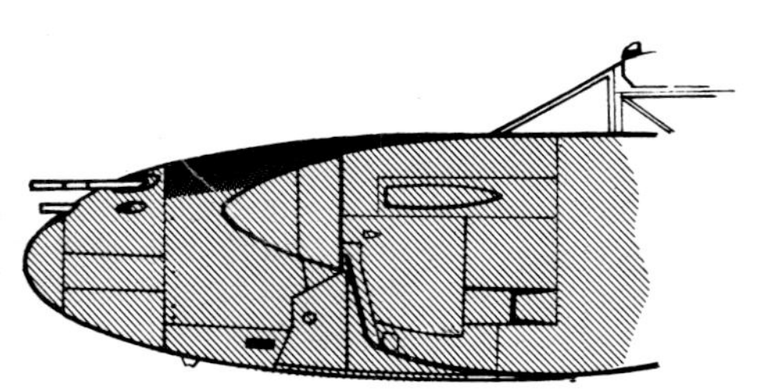

No group colors. Some camouflaged planes had paint removed from spinner & first 12 inches of cowl.

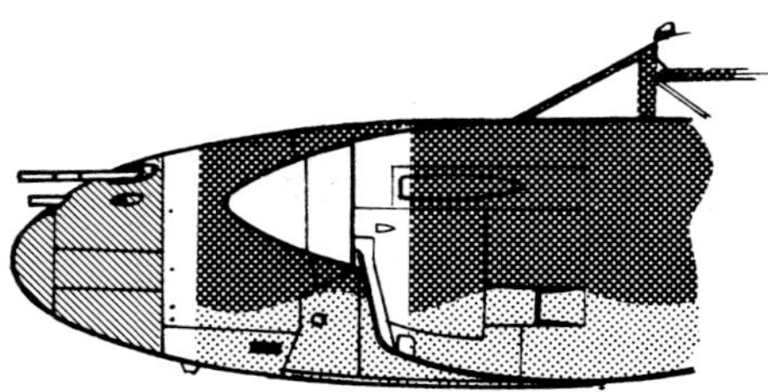

Droop-snoot decoy markings added to many aircraft (from April 1944).

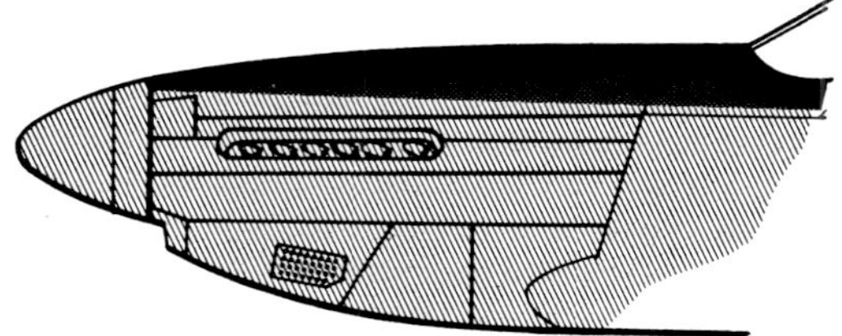

No group color markings on aircraft noses.

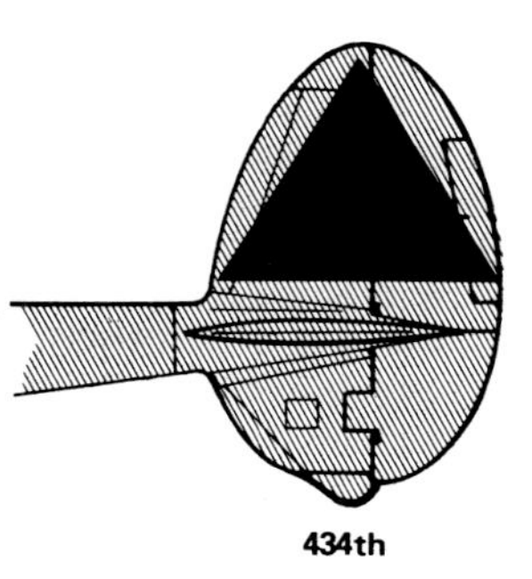

434th

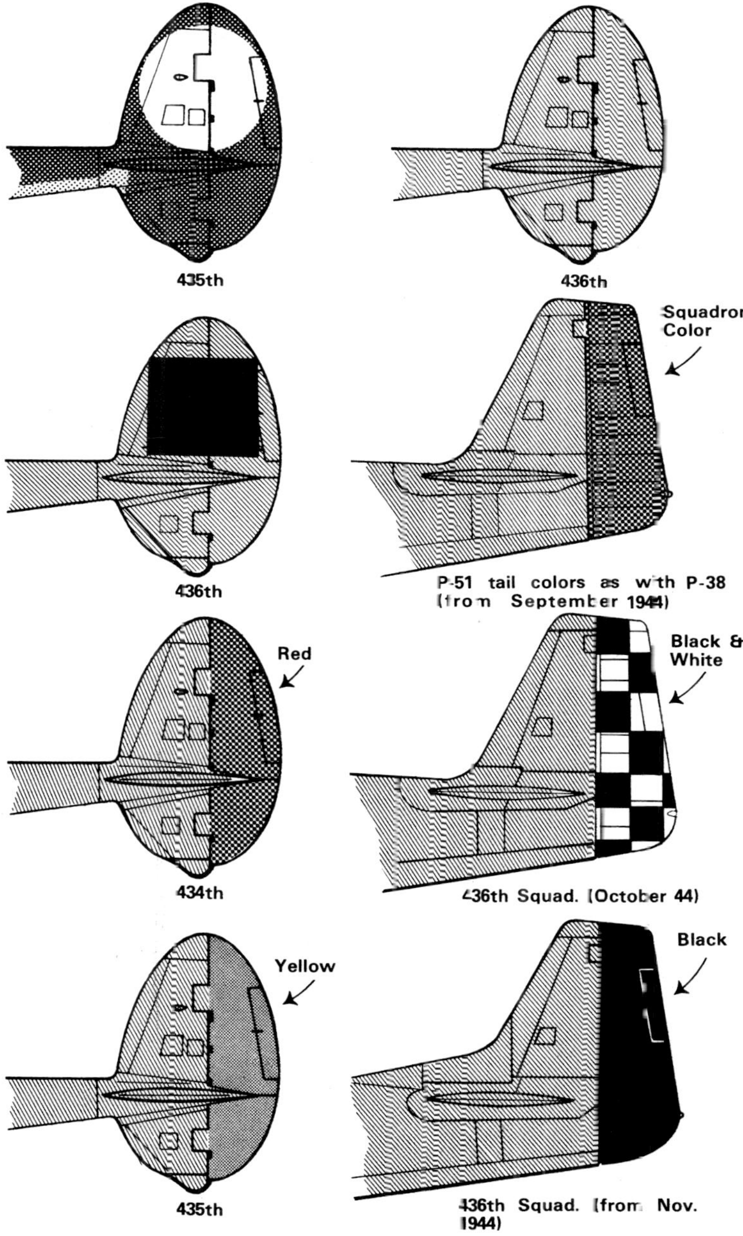

435th

436th

436th

434th

435th

436th

Squadron Color

P-51 tail colors as with P-38 (from September 1944)

Red

Black & White

436th Squad. (October 44)

Yellow

Black

436th Squad. (from Nov. 1944)